Wild and Woolly
KNITTED ANIMALS

A Naturalist's Notebook

Sara Elizabeth Kellner

STACKPOLE
BOOKS

Essex, Connecticut
Blue Ridge Summit, Pennsylvania

T0274226

STACKPOLE BOOKS

An imprint of Globe Pequot, the trade division of
The Rowman & Littlefield Publishing Group, Inc.
4501 Forbes Blvd., Ste. 200
Lanham, MD 20706
www.rowman.com

Distributed by NATIONAL BOOK NETWORK
800-462-6420

Knitting patterns by Sara Elizabeth Kellner
Photography by Sara Elizabeth Kellner and Will Gallagher
Naturalist page illustrations: Pat Kellner
Naturalist page handwriting and layout: Bonnie Kuhl
Flower photo and laurel wreath illustration created by rawpixel.com / Freepik
Art © Getty Images: stephanie phillips / four leaf clovers; ulimi / leaf stamps;
aarud / silver respberry leaves; Goldfinch4ever / pressed pansy flowers;
svrid79 / pressed and dried flowers

British Library Cataloguing in Publication Information available

Library of Congress Cataloging-in-Publication Data

Names: Kellner, Sara Elizabeth, author.
Title: Wild and woolly knitted animals : a naturalist's notebook / Sara
    Elizabeth Kellner.
Description: Guilford, Connecticut : Stackpole Books, [2022] | Summary: "As
    you explore this knitter/naturalist's notebook, you'll learn about the
    creatures she discovers and see her sketches, notes, and knitting
    patterns for each animal. Each animal is portrayed realistically, yet
    endearingly, from a leaping cottontail to a howling timberwolf—25 wild
    animals in all"— Provided by publisher.
Identifiers: LCCN 2021055922 (print) | LCCN 2021055923 (ebook) | ISBN
    9780811771061 (paperback) | ISBN 9780811771078 (epub)
Subjects: LCSH: Knitting—Patterns. | Animals in art.
Classification: LCC TT825 .K444 2022 (print) | LCC TT825 (ebook) | DDC
    746.43/2041—dc23/eng/20211116
LC record available at https://lccn.loc.gov/2021055922
LC ebook record available at https://lccn.loc.gov/2021055923

♾™ The paper used in this publication meets the minimum requirements
of American National Standard for Information Sciences—Permanence of
Paper for Printed Library Materials, ANSI/NISO Z39.48-1992.

First Edition

To my mom,
who always encouraged
creativity
and pointed out
the beauty in nature

Contents

Foreword by Tanis Gray viii

Introduction ix

Abbreviations x

Yarn and Gauge; Stuffing xi

PATTERNS 1

Acknowledgments 163

Contributors 164

1
Mexican
Prairie Dog

7
Rainbow
Trout

15
European
Badger

21
Bald Eagle

27
Red Squirrel

33
Mallard Duck

39
Black-Tailed
Jackrabbit

47
Flatback
Sea Turtle

53
Baby Flatback
Sea Turtle

57
Nest and Eggs of
Black-Headed
Bunting

61
Common
Raccoon

69
Grizzly Bear

75
Chimpanzee

81
Eastern
Gray Squirrel

87
Goliath Frog

97
Brown Rat

103
American
Bison

109
European
Hedgehog

115
Eastern
Cottontail
Rabbit

123
Western
Meadowlark

129
Timber Wolf

135
Asian
Elephant

143
Baby Asian
Elephant

149
Wood Pigeon

155
North American
River Otter

Foreword

Part nature guide, part naturalist's journal, the handknit whimsical creations from Sara Elizabeth Kellner will make your imagination (and knitting needles) run wild!

I've been fortunate enough to work with Sara many times over the years, and no one creates knitted creatures with such accuracy and precision (often with a bit of cheekiness thrown in) like her. The ability to think and create in three dimensions with needles and fiber is a unique one. The gentle curve of a Baby Flatback Sea Turtle's shell, the mischievous face of a Common Raccoon, or the elegant neck of a Wood Pigeon are familiar, and yet, when transformed into woolen versions with our very own hands and this book, we create a unique connection to the animals, gaining intimate knowledge of their shape and movement, their joints, wings, fins, and tails. We learn more about them the way a scientist or zoologist would because of these 25 bewitching patterns.

Many of the creatures in this book are ones we see often, depending on where we live. Some of these critters live in my very own backyard (and quite possibly yours), with still more in the city zoo. Rarely can we get up close and personal with any of them; yet with Sara's patterns, accompanied by charming illustrations with scientific notes created by her own children, Pat and Bonnie, we are able to generate a cozy menagerie of our own. Only in Sara's world can a Red Squirrel be a companion to a Baby Asian Elephant or an American Bison! Her compilation of creatures ranges from sea to sky, from the great open plains of the United States to the grassland habitats of Southeast Asia, the branches of trees in Africa, and suburban hedgerows in Europe. There's something for every kind of animal lover here!

Often worked in a combination of knitting in the round with flat knitting, Sara's design style always brings one word to mind: clever. Smartly placed short rows, embellishment, or even a touch of intarsia turns a stuffed toy into something magical. I have made several of Sara's creations for my own children, and they love to gather round when it's time to add in the stuffing, watching an oddly shaped pile of knitting turn into an elegant animal that is deemed "perfect" and quickly taken away to be played with. There's love and imagination woven into these designs, and you'll find yourself wanting to cast on for another before you're finished binding off.

Welcome to the inspiring world of *Wild and Woolly Knitted Animals*!

Tanis Gray

Introduction

This is a book of animal knitting patterns, but to me, it's a lot more than that. It's a collaboration with two of my children—Pat, who did the illustrations, and Bonnie, who did the handwriting and layout. How lucky am I? It is also the culmination of a lifelong love of both knitting and animals.

Most of the patterns in this book are worked partially in the round and partially flat. Some of them have intarsia, some have embroidery, and some are worked while holding multiple strands of yarn. Some of them even call for multiple sizes of dpns. These are probably not patterns for someone just learning to knit, but an intermediate knitter or a beginner who can work in the round and is not afraid of learning something new will be fine. Also keep in mind that YouTube is a great resource for any of the techniques that are unfamiliar to you. One thing is for sure: I promise you'll never get bored, because each pattern is different, and there's just something magical about seeing an animal come to life in your hands.

I tried to bring together a true assortment of animals for this book. Some you'll probably never get a chance to see in real life, and others are so common you don't even notice them anymore. Maybe after knitting a wood pigeon, you'll stop and look next time you spot a real one and see for the first time the iridescence of its feathers or that wine-colored breast.

Thanks so much for your interest in my designs. Animals make our world a better, more beautiful place to live in, and it's my hope that while you knit (or even just look through the pages), this book will bring you happiness and greater awareness, appreciation, and love for all the animals out there.

Sara

Abbreviations

CO	cast on
dpn	double-pointed needle
EOR	end of round/row
K	knit
Kfb	knit in the front and back of the next stitch
K2tog	knit two stitches together
K2toglp	make a loop out of the K2tog being worked
lp	loop stitch
M1	make 1 stitch*
M1L	make one stitch to the left
M1P	purl the bar between stitches
M1R	make one stitch to the right
P	purl
PSSO	pass slipped stitch over last stitch worked
PU	pick up and knit a new stitch from existing work
PUP	pick up and purl a new stitch from existing work
RS	right side of work
SSK	slip 2 sts k-wise, place back onto left dpn; then K2tog through back loop
SSKlp	make a loop out of the SSK being worked
st	stitch
sts	stitches
w&t	wrap and turn*
WiP	work in pattern
WS	wrong side of work
yo	yarn over

*See further explanation at right.

M1 (MAKE 1 ST)

Lift right leg in row below the next stitch, place on left needle, and knit as any other stitch.

W&T (WRAP AND TURN)

After knitting the specified number of stitches, bring yarn to the front of work, slip the next st on the left dpn to the right one, move yarn to the back of your work, and slip the stitch back to the left needle. This "wraps" the stitch. Turn your work and purl the number of stitches indicated. Bring yarn to the back of work, slip the next st on the left dpn to the right one, move yarn to the front of your work, and slip the stitch back to the left needle. This wraps the second stitch. Turn work and knit the number indicated.

Picking up and knitting the wraps is optional in these patterns. I usually don't pick up any of them. There are a couple of places in this book, though, where I do recommend doing so, and I wrote it into the pattern.

Yarn and Gauge; Stuffing

I used Cascade Aereo and Cascade 220 for projects throughout, at the gauges listed below. Gauge is measured on unblocked swatches worked flat in stockinette stitch.

CASCADE AEREO / CASCADE AEREO DUO

Worked in US size 5/3.75 mm needles
18 sts = 4 inches horizontally
15 rows = 2 inches vertically

CASCADE 220 / CASCADE 220 MERINO

Worked in US size 3/3.25 mm needles
24 sts = 4 inches horizontally
30 rows = 4 inches vertically

I used a particular type of stuffing for every animal in this book. It's called Morning Glory Cluster Stuff polyester fiber.

Gauge is nothing to stress about when it comes to knitting stuffed toys. As long as it is tight enough so that the stuffing doesn't show through the stitches of the finished object, you'll be fine.

There were once billions of prairie dogs across the prairies of mexico, but treatment as an agricultural pest has made them an endangered species. Today there is only a fraction of the original population left.

Conservation groups in mexico are working to restore the population.

MEXICAN PRAIRIE DOG

Sighted at El Tokio Grasslands, Mexico

Prairie dogs have strong muscles in their arms which help them dig through dense dirt.

mexican prairie dogs live in excavated colonies called towns, which they dig for shelter and protection

They have one of the most sophisticated languages in the animal world — high-pitched yips and barks, and they can run up to 35 miles per hour.

Mexican Prairie Dog

SIZE

7.5"/19 cm head to toe
3"/7.5 cm wide

YARN

Cascade Aereo, #4 medium weight, 47% merino
wool/31% baby alpaca/22% nylon, 240 yd./220 m
per 3.5 oz./100 g skein
- A: 08 Camel (body, head, arms, legs);
  100 yd./91 m
- B: 01 Jet (embroidery on face, toes, tip of tail);
  5 yd./4.5 m

NEEDLES

US size 5/3.75 mm dpns

NOTIONS

Darning needle
Stuffing

INSTRUCTIONS

• Body

Work begins at center/back of neckline. With
color A, CO 21 sts onto 3 dpns. Join in the round
by slipping the first CO st onto the 3rd needle
and then pulling the 2nd stitch (formerly the last
st) over it and off the needle; 20 sts remain.
Rnd 1: K all sts.
Rnd 2: (K4, M1R, K4, M1L) 2 times, K4. (24 sts)
Rnd 3: K all sts.
Rnd 4: (K4, M1R, K6, M1L) 2 times, K4. (28 sts)
Rnd 5: K all sts.
Rnd 6: (K4, M1R, K8, M1L) 2 times, K4. (32 sts)
Rnd 7: K all sts.
Rnd 8: (K4, M1R, K10, M1L) 2 times, K4. (36 sts)
Rnds 9–10: K all sts.
Rnd 11: K4, M1R, K3, place 6 sts on scrap yarn, K3,
  M1L, K4, M1R, K3, place 6 sts on scrap yarn, K3,
  M1L, K4. (28 sts)
Rnds 12–13: K all sts.
Rnd 14: K5, M1R, K6, M1L, K6, M1R, K6, M1L, K5.
  (32 sts)
Rnds 15–16: K all sts.
Rnd 17: K5, M1R, K8, M1L, K6, M1R, K8, M1L, K5.
  (36 sts)
Rnds 18–19: K all sts.
Rnd 20: K5, M1R, K10, M1L, K6, M1R, K10, M1L, K5.
  (40 sts)
Rnds 21–41: K all sts.

• Base

Continuing from the body sts.
Rnd 1: (K2tog, K3) 8 times. (32 sts)
Rnd 2: K all sts.
Rnd 3: (K2tog, K2) 8 times. (24 sts)
Rnd 4: K all sts.
Rnd 5: (K2tog, K1) 8 times. (16 sts)
Rnd 6: K all sts.
Rnd 7: (K2tog) 8 times. (8 sts)
  Cut yarn, thread through remaining live sts, and
pull closed. Weave in loose ends.

• Right Arm

Setup: Using the CO tail to identify front of body (CO tail is in the back), place 6 sts from scrap yarn at right side of body onto 2 dpns. With RS facing, rejoin color A at 4th st; K3. With a 3rd dpn, PU 6 new sts around edge of underarm opening; K3 (EOR).

Rnds 1–2: K all sts. (12 sts)
Row 3: K9, w&t.
Row 4: P2, w&t.
Row 5: K3, w&t.
Row 6: P4, w&t.
Row 7: K6 (EOR).
Rnd 8: K2, SSK, K2tog, K6. (10 sts)
Rnds 9–10: K all sts.
Rnd 11: K1, SSK, K2tog, K5. (8 sts)
Rnds 12–13: K all sts.
Rnd 14: SSK, K2tog, K4. (6 sts)
Rnds 15–18: K all sts.

Cut yarn, thread through remaining live sts, and pull closed. Weave in loose ends.

• Left Arm

Repeat all setup instructions as for the right arm.

Rnds 1–2: K all sts. (12 sts)
Row 3: K5, w&t.
Row 4: P2, w&t.
Row 5: K3, w&t.
Row 6: P4, w&t.
Row 7: K10 (EOR).
Rnd 8: K6, SSK, K2tog, K2. (10 sts)
Rnds 9–10: K all sts.
Rnd 11: K5, SSK, K2tog, K1. (8 sts)
Rnds 12–13: K all sts.
Rnd 14: K4, SSK, K2tog. (6 sts)
Rnds 15–18: K all sts.

Cut yarn, thread through remaining live sts, and pull closed. Weave in loose ends. Stuff body and arms; hands are left unstuffed and flattened.

• Head

Setup: Beginning with the first CO st at center/back of neck, PU 20 sts in the original CO sts with color A. Stuff head as you go.

Rnd 1: K all sts.

Rnd 2: (M1, K5) 4 times. (24 sts)

Rnds 3–4: K all sts.

Row 5: K3, w&t.

Row 6: P6, w&t.

Row 7: K7, w&t.

Row 8: P8, w&t.

Row 9: K9, w&t.

Row 10: P10, w&t.

Row 11: K11, w&t.

Row 12: P12, w&t.

Row 13: K6 (EOR).

Rnd 14: (K2tog, K4) 4 times. (20 sts)

Row 15: K2, w&t.

Row 16: P4, w&t.

Row 17: K5, w&t.

Row 18: P6, w&t.

Row 19: K7, w&t.

Row 20: P8, w&t.

Row 21: K9, w&t.

Row 22: P10, w&t.

Row 23: K5 (EOR).

Rnd 24: (K2tog, K3) 4 times. (16 sts)

Rnd 25: K all sts.

Rnd 26: (K2tog, K2) 4 times. (12 sts)

Rnds 27–28: K all sts.

Rnd 29: (K2tog, K1) 4 times. (8 sts)

Before closing the top of head, be sure to add more stuffing if needed. Cut yarn, thread through remaining live sts, and pull closed. Weave in loose ends.

The ears of the Mexican prairie dogs are barely visible on the real animals. With color A, embroider 3 small lines about ½"/1.25 cm long on top of each other running vertically at back/sides of head; then insert darning needle beneath the lines a few times to wrap them and hold together. Weave in loose ends.

• Legs

The top of the legs is created by embroidering a running stitch with color A from the base up 1.5"/3.8 cm and then curving it toward the outside of the body, ending at midway point on

body. Insert darning needle with yarn back down into the body, go through the stuffing, and pull it out near beginning of the running stitch. Pull both ends slightly to cinch and create a gathering, accentuating the top of the legs. Tie a double knot with the 2 ends; weave in loose ends. Repeat on other side.

• Feet

CO 8 sts onto 3 dpns and join in the round by same method used for body; 7 sts remain. K all sts for 10 rounds; cast off. Use CO tail to close tip of foot. With color B, embroider 3 lines about 1.5"/3.8 cm long at CO end of foot to create toes. Seam to bottom of leg with toes sticking out the front. Feet are not stuffed.

• Tail

With color A, CO 4 sts onto 1 dpn, leaving a tail for seaming to body. Work a 4-st I-cord for 10 rows. Cut color A; join color B. Work a 4-st I-cord for 6 rows. Cut yarn, thread through live sts, and pull closed. Weave in loose ends. Seam CO end to back of body just above the base with CO tail. Tail is not stuffed.

• Finishing

Arms are tacked down to sides or in the front with color A.

Embroider eyes on sides of head with color B; these can be small, straight lines above and in front of the ears. The nose is also embroidered with color B.

Freshwater stream rainbow trout average between 1 and 5 lbs.

RAINBOW TROUT

Sighted at Stevens Creek Mountain View California

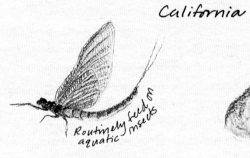

Routinely feed on aquatic insects

The native range is in the coastal waters and tributary streams of the Pacific Basin.

They are distinguished by a broad reddish stripe along the lateral line from gills to tail; most vivid in breeding males.

Since 1875, the rainbow trout has been introduced into river environments throughout the United States and around the world.

Rainbow Trout

SIZE

14"/35.5 cm head to tail
4"/10 cm wide

YARN

Cascade 220, #4 medium weight, 100%
Peruvian Highland wool, 220 yd./200 m per
3.5 oz./100 g skein
- A: 9407 Celery (top of head and body, fins); 50 yd./45.5 m
- B: 7804 Shrimp (horizontal stripe); 20 yd./18 m
- C: 8010 Natural (bottom of head and body); 30 yd./27.5 m
- D: 8555 Black (embroidered spots); 3 yd./2.75 m

NEEDLES

US size 3/3.25 mm dpns

NOTIONS

12 mm fishy safety eyes
Darning needle
Stitch marker (optional)
Stuffing

INSTRUCTIONS

• Head (top)

The head and body are worked flat; turn work after each row. With color A, CO 26 sts onto 1 dpn. The first 7 rows create the trout's inner lip. Rows 8-32 are short rows to shape the head.

Row 1 (WS): P all sts.
Row 2 (RS): K all sts.
Row 3: P all sts.
Row 4: K all sts.
Row 5: P all sts.
Row 6: K all sts.
Row 7: P all sts.
Row 8: K14, w&t.
Row 9: P2, w&t.
Row 10: K3, w&t.
Row 11: P4, w&t.
Row 12: K5, w&t.
Row 13: P6, w&t.

Row 14: K7, w&t.
Row 15: P8, w&t.
Row 16: K9, w&t.
Row 17: P10, w&t.
Row 18: K11, w&t.
Row 19: P12, w&t.
Row 20: K13, w&t.
Row 21: P14, w&t.
Row 22: K15, w&t.
Row 23: P16, w&t.
Row 24: K17, w&t.
Row 25: P18, w&t.
Row 26: K19, w&t.
Row 27: P20, w&t.
Row 28: K21, w&t.
Row 29: P22, w&t.
Row 30: K23, w&t.
Row 31: P24, w&t.
Row 32: K25 (EOR).
Row 33: P all sts.

• Body (top)

Color B is now added to each side of color A to create the horizontal stripes on the sides of the trout. This is done with the intarsia method of colorwork. Begin by preparing a second ball of color B, so you'll have 1 for each side; it only needs to be about 10 yards. When changing colors, always bring the new color over the old one to prevent a gap from forming between them.

Row 1: Color B: K1 (1 st); Color A: M1R, K24, M1L (26 sts); Color B: K1 (1 st).
Row 2: Color B: P1; Color A: P26; Color B: P1.
Row 3: Color B: K2 (2 sts); Color A: M1R, K24, M1L (26 sts); Color B: K2 (2 sts).
Row 4: Color B: P2; Color A: P26; Color B: P2.
Row 5: Color B: K3 (3 sts); Color A: M1R, K24, M1L (26 sts); Color B: K3 (3 sts).
Row 6: Color B: P3; Color A: P26; Color B: P3.
Row 7: Color B: K4 (4 sts); Color A: K24 (24 sts); Color B: K4 (4 sts).

Rows 8-34 are worked in straight stockinette st with the same color combination (4-24-4) as row 7 above. P all sts on the WS, and K all sts on the RS.

Some of the rows in the remainder of the body are short rows to shape the curve in the trout's tail. On those rows, only some of the color A sts are worked, and only one color B stripe is worked. Turn your work and purl back after each of the short rows.

Row 35: Color B: K4; Color A: K2tog, K20, SSK (22 sts); Color B: K4.

Row 36: Color B: P4; Color A: P22; Color B: P4.

Row 37: Color B: K4; Color A: K8, w&t.

Row 38: Color A: P8; Color B: P4.

Row 39: Color B: K4; Color A: K22; Color B: K4.

Row 40: Color B: P4; Color A: P22; Color B: P4.

Row 41: Color B: K4; Color A: K8, w&t.

Row 42: Color A: P8; Color B: P4.

Row 43: Color B: K4; Color A: K22; Color B: K4.

Row 44: Color B: P4; Color A: P22; Color B: P4.

Row 45: Color B: K4; Color A: K2tog, K18, SSK (20 sts); Color B: K4.

Row 46: Color B: P4; Color A: P20; Color B: P4.

Row 47: Color B: K4; Color A: K7, w&t.

Row 48: Color A: P7; Color B: P4.

Row 49: Color B: K4; Color A: K20; Color B: K4.

Row 50: Color B: P4; Color A: P20; Color B: P4.

Row 51: Color B: K4; Color A: K7, w&t.

Row 52: Color A: P7; Color B: P4.

Row 53: Color B: K4; Color A: K20; Color B: K4.

Row 54: Color B: P4; Color A: P20; Color B: P4.

Row 55: Color B: K4; Color A: K2tog, K16, SSK (18 sts); Color B: K4.

Row 56: Color B: P4; Color A: P18; Color B: P4.

Row 57: Color B: K4; Color A: K6, w&t.

Row 58: Color A: P6; Color B: P4.

Row 59: Color B: K4; Color A: K18; Color B: K4.

Row 60: Color B: P4; Color A: P18; Color A: P4.

Row 61: Color B: K4; Color A: K6, w&t.

Row 62: Color A: P6; Color B: P4.

Row 63: Color B: K4; Color A: K18; Color B: K4.

Row 64: Color B: P4; Color A: P18; Color B: P4.

Row 65: Color B: K4; Color A: K2tog, K14, SSK (16 sts); Color B: K4.

Row 66: Color B: P4; Color A: P16; Color B: P4.

Row 67: Color B: K4; Color A: K5, w&t.
Row 68: Color A: P5; Color B: P4.
Row 69: Color B: K4; Color A: K16; Color B: K4.
Row 70: Color B: P4; Color A: P16; Color B: P4.
Row 71: Color B: K4; Color A: K5, w&t.
Row 72: Color A: P5; Color B: P4.
Row 73: Color B: K4; Color A: K16; Color B: K4.
Row 74: Color B: P4; Color A: P16; Color B: P4.
Row 75: Color B: K4; Color A: K2tog, K12, SSK (14 sts); Color B: K4.
Row 76: Color B: P4; Color A: P14; Color B: P4.
Row 77: Color B: K4; Color A: K4, w&t.
Row 78: Color A: P4; Color B: P4.
Row 79: Color B: K4; Color A: K14; Color B: K4.
Row 80: Color B: P4; Color A: P14; Color B: P4.
Row 81: Color B: K4; Color A: K4, w&t.
Row 82: Color A: P4; Color B: P4.
Row 83: Color B: K4; Color A: K14; Color B: K4.
Row 84: Color B: P4; Color A: P14; Color B: P4.
Row 85: Color B: K4; Color A: K2tog, K10, SSK (12 sts); Color B: K4.
Row 86: Color B: P4; Color A: P12; Color B: P4.
Row 87: Color B: K4; Color A: K3, w&t.
Row 88: Color A: P3; Color B: P3.
Row 89: Color B: K4; Color A: K12; Color B: K4.
Row 90: Color B: P4; Color A: P12; Color B: P4.
Row 91: Color B: K4; Color A: K3, w&t.
Row 92: Color A: P3; Color B: P4.
Row 93: Color B: K4; Color A: K12; Color B: K4.
Row 94: Color B: P4; Color A: P12; Color B: P4.
Row 95: Color B: K3; Color A: (K2tog) 2 times, K6, (SSK) 2 times (10 sts); Color B: K3.
Row 96: Color B: P3; Color A: P10; Color B: P3.
Row 97: Color B: K2; Color A: (K2tog) 2 times, K4, (SSK) 2 times (8 sts); Color B: K2.
Row 98: Color B: P2; Color A: P8; Color B: P2.
Cut both strands of color B; the last row of body and all of the tail is worked with color A only.
Row 99: K all sts.
Do not cut color A. Leave live sts on dpn; set aside while working the bottom of head and body.

• Head (bottom)

With color C, CO 26 sts onto 1 dpn. Rows 1–33 of the bottom of the head are worked exactly as the top of the head.

• Body (bottom)

Continuing with color C only.
Row 1: K all sts. (26 sts)
Row 2: P all sts.
Row 3: K all sts.
Row 4: P all sts.
Row 5: K all sts.
Row 6: P all sts.
Row 7: K2tog, K22, SSK. (24 sts)
Rows 8–34 are worked in straight stockinette st. P all sts on WS, and K all sts on RS. As with the top of the body, some of the following rows are short rows to create a curve.
Row 35: K2tog, K20, SSK. (22 sts)
Row 36: P all sts.
Row 37: K all sts.
Row 38: P8, w&t.
Row 39: K8.
Row 40: P all sts.
Row 41: K all sts.
Row 42: P8, w&t.
Row 43: K8.
Row 44: P all sts.

Row 45: K2tog, K18, SSK. (20 sts)
Row 46: P all sts.
Row 47: K all sts.
Row 48: P7, w&t.
Row 49: K7.
Row 50: P all sts.
Row 51: K all sts.
Row 52: P7, w&t.
Row 53: K7.
Row 54: P all sts.
Row 55: K2tog, K16, SSK. (18 sts)
Row 56: P all sts.
Row 57: K all sts.
Row 58: P6, w&t.
Row 59: K6.
Row 60: P all sts.
Row 61: K all sts.
Row 62: P6, w&t.
Row 63: K6.
Row 64: P all sts.
Row 65: K2tog, K14, SSK. (16 sts)
Row 66: P all sts.
Row 67: K all sts.
Row 68: P5, w&t.
Row 69: K5.
Row 70: P all sts.
Row 71: K all sts.
Row 72: P5, w&t.
Row 73: K5.
Row 74: P all sts.
Row 75: K2tog, K12, SSK. (14 sts)
Row 76: P all sts.
Row 77: K all sts.
Row 78: P4, w&t.
Row 79: K4.
Row 80: P all sts.
Row 81: K all sts.
Row 82: P4, w&t.
Row 83: K4.
Row 84: P all sts.
Row 85: K2tog, K10, SSK. (12 sts)
Row 86: P all sts.
Row 87: K all sts.
Row 88: P3, w&t.
Row 89: K3.
Row 90: P all sts.
Row 91: K all sts.
Row 92: P3, w&t.
Row 93: K3.
Row 94: P all sts.
Row 95: K all sts.

Row 96: P all sts.
Row 97: K all sts.
Row 98: P all sts.
Row 99: K all sts.
   Cut color C.

• Tail Fin

Sts from top and bottom pieces are now joined together in the round to work the tail fin. Arrange live sts from both pieces onto 3 or 4 dpns. It will make more sense as you proceed to divide them equally over 4, plus 1 working needle, but that's optional. Use the live strand of color A yarn from the top of the body to work the tail fin.

Setup row: K18, place a st marker or arrange the sts on dpns with a break here to designate the new EOR; 24 sts.
Rnds 1–3: K all sts.
Rnd 4: [(M1L, K1) 2 times, K8, (M1R, K1) 2 times] 2 times. (32 sts)
Rnds 5–7: K all sts.
Rnd 8: [(M1L, K1) 2 times, K12, (M1R, K1) 2 times] 2 times. (40 sts)
Rnds 9–12: K all sts.
   Short rows are now worked over the first and last 10 sts of the round.
Row 13: K9, w&t.
Row 14: P18, w&t.

Row 15: K15, w&t.
Row 16: P12, w&t.
Row 17: K9, w&t.
Row 18: P6, w&t.
Row 19: K3 (EOR).
Row 20: K10, picking up and knitting the wraps together with the stitches that were wrapped, when you come to them; turn work.
Row 21: P20, picking up and purling the wraps together with the stitches they wrapped when you come to them; turn work.
Row 22: K10 (EOR).

Cut yarn. Short rows are now worked over the other 20 sts. With RS facing, rejoin color A at 11th st and repeat rows 13–22 as for the other side of the tail.

Arrange 40 sts evenly on 2 dpns, first 20 on 1 and last 20 on the other so that when flattened, the tail fin runs perpendicular to the body.

Close with the Kitchener stitch. When reaching the center gap, continue to other side normally.

After closing the end of the tail, use duplicate stitching on each side to close the center gap. There should not be a hole there, but it should remain the lowest point on the tail fin.

• Seaming, Attaching Eyes, Stuffing, and Embroidering Spots

The top and bottom body pieces are now seamed together from the outside. Beginning at one side of the tail, use color C and seam along edges with a whipstitch, extending all the way up to the last short row on top and bottom of the mouth.

Safety eyes are attached now, about 4 sts up from seam on each side, and about 5 sts apart from each other.

Next, fold both lips inward at the line created by the short row turns; seam inner edge of lips together. Continue seaming with a whipstitch along opposite side of trout, stuffing as you go and ending at the tail.

Use a dpn from the outside to spread stuffing evenly throughout. The head is slightly flattened top to bottom; the sides are slightly flattened side to side. Make a running stitch with color A across the base of the tail to prevent stuffing from entering it.

Add as few or as many spots as you want with color D. These are primarily located on the color A section of the back but can extend down to the color B stripe and into the color C bottom if desired. The tail of a rainbow trout is also usually spotted.

• Fins

All of the fins are worked with color A, in the round, and left unstuffed. Seam to body with the CO edge at location indicated.

• Dorsal Fin (make 1)

Location: Center/back
    CO 28 sts onto 3 dpns and join in the round.
Rnd 1: K all sts.
Rnd 2: K2tog, K24, SSK. (26 sts)
Rnd 3: (K2tog, K9, SSK) 2 times. (22 sts)
Rnd 4: K2tog, K18, SSK. (20 sts)
Rnd 5: (K2tog, K6, SSK) 2 times. (16 sts)
Rnd 6: K2tog, K12, SSK. (14 sts)
Rnd 7: (K2tog, K3, SSK) 2 times. (10 sts)
Rnd 8: K2tog, K6, SSK. (8 sts)
    Cut yarn, thread through remaining live sts, and pull closed. Weave in loose ends.

• Anal Fin (make 1)

Location: Bottom/in front of tail
    CO 24 sts onto 3 dpns and join in the round.
Rnd 1: K all sts.
Rnd 2: (K2tog, K8, SSK) 2 times. (20 sts)
Rnd 3: K all sts.
Rnd 4: (K2tog, K6, SSK) 2 times. (16 sts)
Rnd 5: K all sts.
Rnd 6: (K2tog, K4, SSK) 2 times. (12 sts)
Rnd 7: K all sts.
Rnd 8: (K2tog, K2, SSK) 2 times. (8 sts)
Rnd 9: K all sts.
    Cut yarn, thread through remaining live sts, and pull closed. Weave in loose ends.

• Pelvic Fins (make 2)

Location: Bottom/center of belly
    CO 12 sts onto 3 dpns and join in the round.
Rnds 1–2: K all sts.
Rnd 3: M1L, K11, M1R, K1. (14 sts)
Rnds 4–5: K all sts.
Rnd 6: M1L, K13, M1R, K1. (16 sts)
Rnds 7–8: K all sts.
Rnd 9: M1L, K15, M1R, K1. (18 sts)
Rnd 10: K all sts.
    Arrange sts on 2 dpns (first 9 on one and second 9 on the other); close with the Kitchener stitch. Weave in loose ends.

• Pectoral Fins (make 2)

Location: On sides, near bottom, behind head
    CO 8 sts onto 3 dpns and join in the round.
Rnds 1–3: K all sts.
Rnd 4: M1L, K7, M1R, K1. (10 sts)
Rnds 5–6: K all sts.
Rnd 7: M1L, K9, M1R, K1. (12 sts)
Rnds 8–9: K all sts.
Rnd 10: (K2tog, K2) 3 times. (9 sts)
Rnd 11: K all sts.
Rnd 12: (K2tog, K1) 3 times. (6 sts)
    Cut yarn, thread through remaining live sts, and pull closed.

European badgers burrow. The dens they construct (called setts) are very complex and passed from generation to generation.

EUROPEAN BADGER

Sighted at Bellever Forest Devon England

While normally docile, badgers can become agressive and ferocious when cornered - making it dangerous for preditors to target them.

Setts can be quite large, and sometimes home to multiple families. when this happens, each family has its own passage and nesting chambers.

Prior to their winter sleep, badgers block their sett entrances with dry leaves and earth - and stop leaving their setts once the snow had fallen.

Their muscular and flexable snouts are used for digging and probing.

European Badger

SIZE

14"/35.5 cm nose to tail
6"/15 cm wide

YARN

Cascade Aereo, #4 medium weight, 47% merino wool/31% baby alpaca/22% nylon, 240 yd./220 m per 3.5 oz./100 g skein
- A: 04 Ecru (head, tips of ears); 10 yd./9 m
- B: 01 Jet (head; legs, ears, nose); 30 yd./27.5 m
- C suggestions: 02 Charcoal; 03 Silver; 05 Doeskin Heather; 06 Walnut Heather (body, tail); 150 yd./137 m held double with 1 or 2 colors

NEEDLES

US size 5/3.75 mm dpns
US size 8/5.0 mm dpns

NOTIONS

7 mm round black safety eyes
Darning needle
Stitch marker (optional)
Stuffing

INSTRUCTIONS

• Upper Head

Work begins at tip of snout with a few short rows for shaping. With color A, CO 6 sts onto 1 smaller-size dpn. Rows are worked flat.

Row (WS) 1: P6.
Row (RS) 2: K4, w&t.
Row 3: P2, w&t.
Row 4: K3, w&t.
Row 5: P4, w&t.
Row 6: K5 (EOR).

Arrange sts on 2 dpns (3–3) and with 2 other dpns, RS facing and working yarn coming from the top st, PU 6 sts around edges of work: 1 st along each edge and 4 sts along the CO side. K3 (new EOR). Turn work, slip 1, P11. Measure off 3 yards of yarn, and then cut.

The remainder of the head continues to be worked flat, using the intarsia method of colorwork and 5 strands of yarn. Measure and cut 2 strands of color B, each 3 yards long, and 2 additional strands of color A, each 3 yards long. These strands are not rolled into balls; rather, they are left long and draped over the arm of your chair or other surface so that they can easily be untangled if need be while working.

When changing colors, always bring the new color over the old one to prevent a gap from forming between them. In Row 1, all of the strands of yarn are brought into the work. The very first color A will be the same strand you used to shape the snout. After that, grab each strand as it is needed.

Row 1: Color A: Slip 1, K2; Color B: K2; Color A: K2; Color B: K2; Color A: K3.
Row 2: Color A: Slip 1, P2; Color B: P2; Color A: P2; Color B: P2; Color A: P3.
Row 3: Color A: Slip 1, K2; Color B: K2; Color A: K2; Color B: K2; Color A: K3.
Row 4: Color A: Slip 1, P2; Color B: P2; Color A: P2; Color B: P2; Color A: P3.
Row 5: Color A: Slip 1, K2; Color B: K2; Color A: K2; Color B: K2; Color A: K3.
Row 6: Color A: Slip 1, P2; Color B: P2; Color A: P2; Color B: P2; Color A: P3.
Row 7: Color A: Slip 1, M1R, K2 (4 sts); Color B: K2; Color A: K1, M1R, K1 (3 sts); Color B: K2; Color A: K2, M1L, K1 (4 sts).
Row 8: Color A: Slip 1, P3; Color B: P2; Color A: P3; Color B: P2; Color A: P4.
Row 9: Color A: Slip 1, K3; Color B: K2; Color A: K3; Color B: K2; Color A: K4.
Row 10: Color A: Slip 1, P3; Color B: P2; Color A: P3; Color B: P2; Color A: P4.
Row 11: Color A: Slip 1, K3; Color B: K1, M1R, K1 (3 sts); Color A: K2, M1L, K1 (4 sts); Color B: K1, M1L, K1 (3 sts); Color A: K4.
Row 12: Color A: Slip 1, P3; Color B: P3; Color A: P4; Color B: P3; Color A: P4.
Row 13: Color A: Slip 1, M1R, K3 (5 sts); Color B: K3; Color A: K4; Color B: K3; Color A: K3, M1L, K1 (5 sts).
Row 14: Color A: Slip 1, P4; Color B: P3; Color A: P4; Color B: P3; Color A: P5.
Row 15: Color A: Slip 1, K4; Color B: K3; Color A: K4; Color B: K3; Color A: K5.

Row 16: Color A: Slip 1, P4; Color B: P3; Color A: P4; Color B: P3; Color A: P5.

Row 17: Color A: Slip 1, M1R, K4 (6 sts); Color B: K1, M1R, K2 (4 sts); Color A: K4; Color B: K2, M1L, K1 (4 sts); Color A: K4, M1L, K1 (6 sts).

Row 18: Color A: Slip 1, P5; Color B: P4; Color A: P4; Color B: P4; Color A: P6.

Row 19: Color A: Slip 1, K5; Color B: K4; Color A: K4; Color B: K4; Color A: K6.

Row 20: Color A: Slip 1, P5; Color B: P4; Color A: P4; Color B: P4; Color A: P6.

Row 21: Color A: Slip 1, K5; Color B: K4; Color A: K4; Color B: K4; Color A: K6.

Row 22: Color A: Slip 1, P5; Color B: P4; Color A: P4; Color B: P4; Color A: P6.

Rows 23–29 are short rows to shape the top of the head. Always wrap sts with the same color as the stitches being wrapped. All sts are worked using the same colors as row 22 for the remainder of the head.

Row 23: Slip 1, K13, w&t.
Row 24: P4, w&t.
Row 25: K5, w&t.
Row 26: P6, w&t.
Row 27: K7, w&t.
Row 28: P8, w&t.
Row 29: K16 (EOR).
Row 30: Slip 1, P23.
Row 31: Slip 1, K23.
Row 32: Slip 1, P23.
Row 33: Slip 1, K23.

Place live sts on a piece of scrap yarn. With color A, seam rows 1 and 2 together at the bottom to create a round snout. Trim all strands of yarn to 2–3 inches. These are left tucked inside the head.

• Lower Head

With color B, CO 3 sts to 1 smaller-size dpn and work the following rows back and forth.

Row 1: P all sts.
Row 2: K all sts.
Row 3: P all sts.
Row 4: Slip 1, M1R, K2. (4 sts)
Row 5: Slip 1, P3.
Row 6: Slip 1, K3.
Row 7: Slip 1, P3.
Row 8: Slip 1, M1R, K2, M1L, K1. (6 sts)
Row 9: Slip 1, P5.
Row 10: Slip 1, M1R, K4, M1L, K1. (8 sts)
Row 11: Slip 1, P7.
Row 12: Slip 1, K7.

Row 13: Slip 1, P7.
Row 14: Slip 1, M1R, K6, M1L, K1. (10 sts)
Row 15: Slip 1, P9.
Row 16: Slip 1, K9.
Row 17: Slip 1, P9.
Row 18: Slip 1, M1R, K8, M1L, K1. (12 sts)
Row 19: Slip 1, P11.
Row 20: Slip 1, K11.
Row 21: Slip 1, P11.
Row 22: Slip 1, M1R, K10, M1L, K1. (14 sts)
Row 23: Slip 1, P13.
Row 24: Slip 1, K13.
Row 25: Slip 1, P13.
Row 26: Slip 1, K13.
Row 27: Slip 1, P13.

Leave live sts on dpn; do not break yarn. With right sides facing outward, fit lower head inside of upper head, and with color B, seam edges together from front to back using a whipstitch.

• Chest

The chest continues from the lower head piece, using color B and smaller dpns. Continue working flat.

Row 1: Slip 1, M1R, K12, M1L, K1. (16 sts)
Row 2: Slip 1, P15.
Row 3: Slip 1, K15.
Row 4: Slip 1, P15.
Row 5: Slip 1, M1R, K14, M1L, K1. (18 sts)
Row 6: Slip 1, P17.
Row 7: Slip 1, K17.
Row 8: Slip 1, P17.
Row 9: Slip 1, M1R, K16, M1L, K1. (20 sts)
Row 10: Slip 1, P19.
Row 11: Slip 1, K19.
Row 12: Slip 1, P19.
Row 13: Slip 1, M1R, K18, M1L, K1. (22 sts)
Row 14: Slip 1, P21.
Row 15: Slip 1, K21.

• Front Legs

Arrange last 11 sts on 3 dpns; place first 11 sts on a piece of scrap yarn. CO 3 new sts to the end of the sts on the needles and join in the round. (14 sts)

Rnds 1–11: K all sts.
Rnd 12: K12 (new EOR).

Add st marker or arrange sts on the dpns with a break here to designate new EOR. Short rows are now worked to shape the back of the heel. Two sts will be wrapped 3 times each. A small hole created by the wraps may need to be seamed closed after stuffing.

Rnd 13: K2, w&t.
Rnd 14: P4, w&t.
Rnd 15: K4, w&t.
Rnd 16: P4, w&t.
Rnd 17: K4, w&t.
Rnd 18: P4, w&t.
Rnd 19: K2 (EOR).
Rnd 20: K5, SSK K2tog, K5. (12 sts)
Rnds 21–26: K all sts.

Cut yarn, thread through live sts, and pull closed. Weave in loose ends.

Place 11 sts from scrap yarn onto 3 dpns and with RS facing, rejoin color B at first st, K11. CO 3 new sts to end of round; join in the round and repeat all instructions as for the other leg.

Safety eyes should now be attached. These are positioned in the center of the color B stripes, about 5–6 rows up from where color B begins.

Stuff legs, using a dpn from the outside to shift stuffing evenly around and accentuating the heel. Feet should have very little stuffing in them and be more flat than round.

Stuff head, which should remain flat on the bottom; add only enough stuffing to the head to make it rounded on the top.

• Body

Live sts at the back of the head are now combined with picked-up sts around the chest and legs to begin the body.

Setup: Place 24 sts from scrap yarn onto 2 larger-size dpns. With color C held double (or 2 different colors) and RS facing, join yarn at 13th st; K12.

PU 10 sts along edge of chest from live sts down to right leg. PU 8 sts across the top of the legs. PU 10 sts from left leg up to live sts, K12; 52 sts (EOR). Join sts in the round.

Rnds 1–30: K all sts.

Short rows are now worked to change direction of the sts and shape the curve in your badger's back.

Row 31: K4, w&t.
Row 32: P8, w&t.
Row 33: K10, w&t.
Row 34: P12, w&t.
Row 35: K14, w&t.
Row 36: P16, w&t.
Row 37: K18, w&t.
Row 38: P20, w&t.
Row 39: K22, w&t.
Row 40: P24, w&t.
Row 41: K26, w&t.
Row 42: P28, w&t.
Row 43: K30, w&t.
Row 44: P32, w&t.
Row 45: K34, w&t.
Row 46: P36, w&t.
Row 47: K38, w&t.
Row 48: P40, w&t.
Row 49: K20 (EOR).
Rnd 50: K50, place last 2 sts on scrap yarn; CO 2 new sts to end of round.
Rnd 51: Place first 2 sts on same piece of scrap yarn; CO 2 new sts to working needle, K50. Repeat short rows 31–46 and then K18 (EOR).

Cut yarn; place all live sts on a piece of scrap yarn while tail is worked.

• Tail

Setup: Place 4 live sts from scrap yarn onto 2 larger-size dpns. With RS facing, join double strand of color C at 3rd st; K2. PU 12 sts around edge of opening; K2; 16 sts total (EOR). Join sts in the round.

Rnds 1–30: K all sts.
Rnd 31: K6, SSK, K2tog, K6. (14 sts)
Rnd 32: K all sts.
Rnd 33: K5, SSK, K2tog, K5. (12 sts)
Rnd 34: K all sts.
Rnd 35: K4, SSK, K2tog, K4. (10 sts)

Cut yarn, thread through remaining live sts, and pull closed. Weave in loose end.

Stuff tail, using a dpn from the outside to shift stuffing evenly around. Do not stuff body at this time, as doing so will make the back legs more difficult to work. The tail will stick out slightly but can be tacked down if desired after working legs and stuffing body.

• Back Right Leg

The back legs are worked with smaller-size dpns and one strand of color B yarn.

Setup: Place first 26 sts from scrap yarn onto 3 dpns. With RS facing, join yarn at former first st in round; K6. Arrange sts on needles with a break or st marker here to designate new EOR; K20; join sts in the round. The remaining 26 sts are left on scrap yarn. K6 (EOR).

Rnds 1–3: K all sts.
Rnd 4: (K2tog, K9, SSK) 2 times. (22 sts)
Rnds 5–6: K all sts.
Rnd 7: (K2tog, K7, SSK) 2 times. (18 sts)
Rnds 8–9: K all sts.
Rnd 10: (K2tog, K5, SSK) 2 times. (14 sts)
Rnds 11–14: K all sts.

Repeat rounds 13–26 of the front legs. Cut yarn, thread through remaining live sts, and pull closed. Weave in loose ends.

• Back Left Leg

The back left leg is worked the same as the Back Right Leg after the initial setup. Place 26 sts from scrap yarn onto 3 dpns. Join color B at next st in round (at bottom of badger); K20 (new EOR). Arrange sts on needles with a break or st marker here. K 1 round; then repeat rounds 1–14 the same as for the right leg, as well as rounds 13–26 of the front legs.

• Ears

With smaller-size needles and color B yarn, CO 6 sts onto 1 dpn. The ears are worked flat.

Row 1: P all sts.
Row 2: K all sts.
Row 3: P all sts.
Row 4: SSK, (K2tog) 2 times. (3 sts)

Cut yarn, thread through remaining live sts, and pull closed. Weave in loose end. The edges of the ears are wrapped with color A and a darning needle. Use CO tail to seam to head on color B stripe in a cupped position, about 3–4 rows from the back of head.

Stuff body and back legs/feet fully now through hole between legs. Use a dpn from the outside to shift stuffing evenly.

The hole is then held together front to back and seamed closed with color C.

Nose is embroidered with color B.

BALD EAGLE

Sighted at Erik Hansen Scout Park Kenai, Alaska

To hunt fish, the eagle swoops down over the water and snatches fish with its talons. They eat by holding the fish in one claw and tearing the flesh with the other.

Bald Eagle's natural range covers most of North America, Including most of Canada, all of the Continental United States, and northern Mexico.

The beak, feet, and irises are bright yellow.

wingspan is between 5ft 11in and 7ft 7in

Females are about 25% larger than males

Bald Eagle

SIZE

13"/33 cm head to toe
6"/15 cm wide

YARN

Cascade Aereo, #4 medium weight, 47% merino wool/31% baby alpaca/22% nylon, 240 yd./220 m per 3.5 oz./100 g skein
- A: 07 Mocha Heather (body, upper legs, wings); 150 yd./137 m
- B: 04 Ecru (head, tail feathers); 50 yd./45.5 m

Cascade Ultra Pima, #3 light weight, 100% Pima cotton, 220 yd./200 m per 3.5 oz./100 g skein
- C: 3747 Gold (beak, lower legs, toes); 10 yd./9 m
- D: 3754 True Black (talons); 2 yd./2 m

NEEDLES

US size 5/3.75 mm dpns

NOTIONS

8 mm yellow safety eyes
Darning needle
Stuffing

INSTRUCTIONS

• Body

Work begins at center/back of neckline. With color A, CO 33 sts onto 3 dpns. Join in the round by slipping the first CO st onto the 3rd needle and then pulling the 2nd stitch (formerly the last st) over it and off the needle; 32 sts remain. Rounds 8-10 are short rows worked over just some of the sts. Knitting in the round resumes on round 11.

Rnds 1–3: K all sts.
Rnd 4: K4, (M1, K3) 4 times, (K3, M1) 4 times, K4. (40 sts)
Rnd 5: K all sts.
Rnd 6: K4, (M1, K4) 4 times, (K4, M1) 4 times, K4. (48 sts)
Rnd 7: K all sts.
Rnd 8: K32, w&t.
Rnd 9: P16, w&t.
Rnd 10: K32.
Rnds 11–15: K all sts.
  Repeat rounds 8–15 five more times.

• Upper Legs

K24, place next 24 plus first 6 sts on a piece of scrap yarn; 18 sts remain. Arrange these 18 sts on 3 dpns and join in the round; K 8 rounds and then cast off all sts using the following variation of the picot cast-off.

PICOT CAST-OFF

1. K2tog, place st back onto left-hand needle.
2. CO 3 new sts on the left needle using the knitted cast-on.
3. Cast off first 3 sts.
4. K2tog.
5. Cast off 2nd st on right-hand needle; place last st on right-hand needle back on the left-hand needle.

  Repeat steps 2–5 seven more times for a total of 8 picots around the bottom of the upper leg. Cut yarn, and thread through last remaining st. Weave in loose ends.

Place 18 stitches from scrap yarn onto 1 dpn; K18. Make sure that the 12 sts remaining on scrap yarn are at the center/back of the body (the 6 stitches on either side of the original EOR). Join 18 sts in the round, and repeat all instructions for the other upper leg.

• Back of Body and Tail Feathers

Back of body: Place 12 sts from scrap yarn onto 2 dpns. With RS facing, rejoin color A at first st, K6 (new EOR). K6, PU 12 sts around edge of opening with 2 more dpns, K6. There should now be 4 dpns with 6 sts on each for a total of 24 sts. K all sts for 4 rounds.

  Tail feathers: Cut color A; join color B. Now work 4 tail feathers one at a time over 6 sts each. K6, place 18 on scrap yarn. Join 6 sts just worked in the round.

Rnd 1: K all sts.
Rnd 2: (M1, K3) 2 times. (8 sts)
Rnds 3–5: K all sts.
Rnd 6: (M1, K4) 2 times. (10 sts)
Rnds 7–9: K all sts.
Rnd 10: (M1, K5) 2 times. (12 sts)

Rnds 11–20: K all sts.
Rnd 21: K2tog, K8, SSK. (10 sts)
Rnd 22: K2tog, K6, SSK. (8 sts)

Cut yarn, thread through live sts, and pull closed. Tail feathers should be left unstuffed and flattened with increases on the sides. Repeat all instructions 3 more times with remaining 18 sts.

The hole between the tail feathers is closed by threading a darning needle with a piece of color A yarn about 12 inches long. Beginning with any feather and leaving a tail, thread it through the base of each feather; then pull both ends snugly to bring all the feathers together and close the hole. Repeat if necessary. Tie a knot with the two ends. Weave in loose ends.

Stuff body.

• Head

Sts are now picked up in the original CO sts to begin the head. Knitter has the option of a front-facing or side-facing head. For front-facing, begin at the center/back of neck. For side-facing, count 8 sts to the left of the center/back st and begin picking up sts there; after that, both heads are worked the same. The M1s in the setup round below can be made through a purl bump on the inside of your work.

Setup: With color B (PU 4, M1) 8 times. (40 sts)
Rnds 1–3: K all sts.
Rnd 4: (K2tog, K8) 4 times. (36 sts)
Rnds 5–6: K all sts.
Rnd 7: (K2tog, K7) 4 times. (32 sts)
Rnds 8–9: K all sts.
Rnd 10: (K2tog, K6) 4 times. (28 sts)

Rows 11–35 below are short rows worked back and forth over just some of the sts at both ends of the round. Working in the round over all the sts resumes in round 36.

Row 11: K9, w&t.
Row 12: P18, w&t.
Row 13: K17, w&t.
Row 14: P16, w&t.
Row 15: K15, w&t.
Row 16: P14, w&t.
Row 17: K13, w&t.
Row 18: P12, w&t.
Row 19: K11, w&t.
Row 20: P10, w&t.
Row 21: K9, w&t.
Row 22: P8, w&t.
Row 23: K7, w&t.

Row 24: P6, w&t.
Row 25: K12, w&t.
Row 26: P18, w&t.
Row 27: K17, w&t.
Row 28: P16, w&t.
Row 29: K15, w&t.
Row 30: P14, w&t.
Row 31: K13, w&t.
Row 32: P12, w&t.
Row 33: K11, w&t.
Row 34: P10, w&t.
Row 35: K5 (EOR).

Add stuffing to the neck and head so far.

Rnd 36: K all sts.
Rnd 37: (K2, K2tog) 3 times, K2tog, SSK, (SSK, K2) 3 times. (20 sts)
Rnd 38: K all sts.
Rnd 39: (K2, K2tog) 2 times, K2tog, SSK, (SSK, K2) 2 times. (14 sts)
Rnd 40: K all sts.
Rnd 41: (K1, K2tog) 2 times, K2, (SSK, K1) 2 times. (10 sts)
Rnd 42: K all sts.

Attach safety eyes now about 4 sts back from the end of color B, and about 8 sts apart from each other on top. Finish stuffing head.

• Beak

Cut color B; join color C held double.
Rnd 1: K all sts. (10 sts)
Rnd 2: K2tog, K6, SSK. (8 sts)
Rnds 3–5: K all sts.
Rnd 6: K2tog, K4, SSK. (6 sts)

Arrange sts on 2 dpns, first 3 on 1 and last 3 on the other. Join with the Kitchener stitch. Pull loose end downward after pulling yarn through last 2 sts. Weave in loose ends. Embroider a tiny "nostril" with color D on both sides.

• Neck Feathers

The division between color A (body) and color B (neck) is softened by embroidering small "feathers" with color B. Thread a darning needle with a piece of color B that is 1–2'/30–61 cm in length; insert into neck area and out ½–1"/1.25–2.5 cm away. Make feathers of varying lengths.

Embroider color B above the eyes, slightly covering the top of the eye, in 2–3 small lines that lie on top of each other, each about ½"/1.25 cm long.

• Lower Legs and Toes (make 2 the same)

Lower legs and toes are worked separately from the body and seamed to the bottom/inside of the upper leg. With color C held double, CO 7 sts onto 3 dpns and join in the round with the same method used for the body; 6 sts remain.
Rnds 1–6: K all sts.
Rnd 7: M1, K1, (M1, K2) 2 times, M1, K1. (10 sts)
Rnds 8–9: K all sts.
Rnd 10: K3, slide 3 sts just worked to the other side of the dpn.

Work a 3-st I-cord for 4 rows. Cut yarn, and thread through sts; pull closed. Weave loose end down one side and push end into base of lower leg. Repeat 2 more times over 3 sts on each side of the first toe; 1 st remains. PU 1 st on each side of it and repeat. Arrange toes so that 3 are pointing in one direction and one is pointing in the opposite direction. Hold in this position and sew together at base with color C.

• Talons

Talons can be made in different ways or simply embroidered.

The method I use: Cut a piece of color D about 8–10 inches long. Thread through the tip of one of the toes; repeat once or twice in same location. Pass darning needle through the tip of the color D loop created before pulling tight, similar to a chain stitch in crochet. Repeat 2–3 times until talon is about ¼"/7 mm long. Weave in loose ends.

Insert the top of the lower leg into the upper leg ½"/1.25 cm, and seam in place with color A. A gap between the upper and the lower legs in the back is fine and looks realistic, but if you'd like to close the bottom of the upper leg, this can be done by running a gathering stitch just above the picot bind-off to pull the upper legs tight around the lower leg, closing the opening.

• Wings (make 2 the same)

The wings are worked separately and seamed to the body. The first part is worked flat. CO 11 sts to 1 dpn.
Row 1: P all sts.
Row 2: K all sts.
Row 3: P all sts.
Row 4: K7, w&t.
Row 5: P3, w&t.
Row 6: K4, w&t.
Row 7: P5, w&t.
Row 8: K6, w&t.
Row 9: P7, w&t.
Row 10: K9 (EOR).
Row 11: P all sts.
Row 12: K all sts.

Rnd 29: K4, P1, K8, P1, K22.
Rnd 30: K5, P1, K6, P1, K23.
Rnd 31: K6, P1, K4, P1, K24.
Rnd 32: K7, P1, K2, P1, K25.
Rnd 33: K1, K2tog, K5, P2, K5, SSK, K2, K2tog, K12, SSK, K1. (32 sts)
Rnd 34: K all sts.
Rnd 35: (K1, K2tog, K10, SSK, K1) 2 times. (28 sts)
Rnd 36: K all sts.
Rnd 37: (K1, K2tog, K8, SSK, K1) 2 times. (24 sts)
Rnd 38: K all sts.
Rnd 39: (K1, K2tog, K6, SSK, K1) 2 times. (20 sts)
Rnd 40: K all sts.
Rnd 41: (K1, K2tog, K4, SSK, K1) 2 times. (16 sts)
Rnd 42: K all sts.
Rnd 43: (K1, K2tog, K2, SSK, K1) 2 times. (12 sts)
Rnd 44: K all sts.
Rnd 45: (K1, K2tog, SSK, K1) 2 times. (8 sts)
Rnd 46: K all sts.

Cut yarn, thread through remaining live sts, and pull closed. Weave in loose ends.

With 1 dpn and RS facing, PU 16 sts along the edge of your knitted piece from the place where the decreases begin down to the point at bottom. PU 16 sts with a 2nd dpn along the opposite side from point at bottom to the place where the decreases begin on that side.

The bottom of the wing is worked in a 3 x 1 rib pattern using a total of 3 dpns:
(RS): (K3, P1)
(WS): (P3, K1)

After picking up 32 sts, turn your work and begin:
Row 1 (WS): Slip 1, P2, K1, (P3, K1) to end.
Row 2 (RS): Slip 1, K1, cast off 2 (the first two sts), WiP to EOR. (30 sts)
Row 3: Slip 1, K1, cast off 2 (the first two sts), WiP to EOR. (28 sts)

Repeat last 2 rows until 4 sts remain. Cut yarn, thread through, and pull closed. Weave in loose ends.

Position wings where you want them on the body and hold or pin in place. The upper curve of the wing can be facing forward or upward at any angle.

Seam to body with color A from the lower purl detail toward the top of the wing about 3"/7.5 cm, and another 3"/7.5 cm in the center of the back of the wing. Place the front seam about ½"/1.25 cm on the inside so it will be hidden. The top and bottom of the wings will be unattached.

Your knitted piece should look like a rectangle with a bump in the middle. Arrange 11 sts onto 2 dpns, 6 on the first one, 5 on the other. The working yarn should come from the last st on the needle with 5 sts.

It's helpful to work the following section with 5 dpns, but it's not necessary. With RS facing, PU 1 st along the edge of work near the last st, and place it at the end of the row. With 2 additional dpns, PU 12 more sts evenly around the edge of the piece, 2 on each side and 8 along the CO edge; 24 sts total. Place a st marker, or arrange sts with a break here to designate the EOR. The remainder of this section is worked in the round.

Rnds 1–3: K all sts.
Rnd 4: (K1, M1R, K10, M1L, K1) 2 times. (28 sts)
Rnds 5–10: K all sts.
Rnd 11: (K1, M1R, K12, M1L, K1) 2 times. (32 sts)
Rnds 12–18: K all sts.
Rnd 19: P1, K14, P1, K16.
Rnd 20: K1, P1, K12, P1, K17.
Rnd 21: K2, P1, K10, P1, K18.
Rnd 22: K1, M1R, K2, P1, K8, P1, K2, M1L, K2, M1R, K14, M1L, K1. (36 sts)
Rnd 23: K5, P1, K6, P1, K23.
Rnd 24: K6, P1, K4, P1, K24.
Rnd 25: P1, K6, P1, K2, P1, K6, P1, K18.
Rnd 26: K1, P1, K6, P2, K6, P1, K19.
Rnd 27: K2, P1, K12, P1, K20.
Rnd 28: K3, P1, K10, P1, K21.

RED SQUIRREL

- Sighted at Blackmurr Wood Strathpeffer, Scotland

The red squirrel has sharp, curved claws to help it climb.

The coat of the red squirrel varies in color with time of year and location. The underside of the squirrel is always white-cream in colour. The red squirrel sheds it's coat twice a year.

The introduction of the grey squirrel from America caused native red squirrel numbers to plummet, perhaps partly due to competition from the larger American, but also due to the squirrel pox virus carried by the greys

hello little squirrel♡

Red Squirrel

SIZE

6.5"/16.5 cm head to tail
3"/7.5 cm wide

YARN

Cascade Aereo, #4 medium weight, 47% merino wool/31% baby alpaca/22% nylon, 240 yd./220 m per 3.5 oz./100 g skein
- A: 17 Provence (body, legs, tail, head); 100 yd./91 m
- B: 04 Ecru (underside); 20 yd./18 m

NEEDLES

US size 5/3.75 mm dpns

NOTIONS

6 mm black round safety eyes
Darning needle
Scrap of light-brown yarn to embroider around eyes
Stuffing
Stitch marker (optional)
Wire pet brush (optional)

INSTRUCTIONS

• Chest

Work begins at neckline. The chest is worked flat with the intarsia method of colorwork. Begin by preparing a second, small ball of color A (about 8–10 yards); then CO the following sts onto 1 dpn:
Color A: CO 7 sts
Color B: CO 2 sts
Color A: CO 7 sts
   Row 1, as well as all odd rows through 11, are purled with the same number of sts and same colors as the prior row.
Row 2: Color A: K7; Color B: K2; Color A: K7.
Row 4: Color A: K1, M1R, K6. (8 sts); Color B: K2; Color A: K6, M1L, K1 (8 sts).
Row 6: Color A: K1, M1R, K7 (9 sts); Color B: K2; Color A: K7, M1L, K1 (9 sts).
Row 8: Color A: K1, M1R, K8 (10 sts); Color B: K1, M1L, K1 (3 sts); Color A: K8, M1L, K1 (10 sts).
Row 10: Color A: K1, M1R, K9 (11 sts); Color B: K3; Color A: K9, M1L, K1 (11 sts).

Row 12: Color A: K1, M1R, K10 (12 sts); Color B: K1, M1R, K2 (4 sts); Color A: K10, M1L, K1 (12 sts).

• Front Left Leg

Arrange last 12 sts onto 3 dpns and join in the round. Place first 16 sts on a piece of scrap yarn. Do not cut any of the working yarns at this point. K9; place st marker or arrange sts with a break here to designate new EOR.
Row 1: K1, w&t.
Row 2: P2, w&t.
Row 3: K3, w&t.
Row 4: P4, w&t.
Row 5: K2 (EOR).
Rnds 6–7: K all sts.
Rnd 8: K2tog, K8, SSK. (10 sts)
Rnds 9–10: K all sts.
Rnd 11: K2tog, K6, SSK. (8 sts)
Rnds 12–13: K all sts.
Rnd 14: K2tog, K4, SSK. (6 sts)
Rnds 15–16: K all sts.
Rnd 17: K2, (M1, K1) 2 times, K2. (8 sts)
Rnds 18–21: K all sts.
   Cut yarn, thread through remaining live sts, and pull closed. Weave in loose ends.

• Front Right Leg

Arrange first 12 sts from scrap yarn onto 3 dpns and join in the round. Leave the 4 color B sts on scrap yarn. Using the working yarn from that section, K3. Place st marker or arrange sts on dpns with a break here to designate new EOR. Work all rows the same as the left leg.

• Body

Seam together the first 3 rows at the top of the chest, forming a circle for the neck opening. Sts are now picked up on the inside of the legs and around the edge of the chest to shape the body.
Setup: With RS facing, flatten the left leg with "elbow" and decreases in a straight line down the back. This will help you see where the center of the inner leg is. Begin on the left side and PU the top 2 sts in the center of the inner left leg, and then PU 10 sts along the left edge of work up to the center/top. With a 2nd dpn, PU 10 sts along right edge of work down to the

right leg, followed by 2 more sts at the top of the center of the inner right leg (24 sts); EOR.

The body is worked flat, turning your work after each row. After 2–3 rows, all sts can be transferred to 1 dpn. Leave the color B sts in the center on scrap yarn for now.

Row 1 and all odd rows through 27 are worked: Slip 1, P23.

Row 2: SSK, K9, M1L, K2, M1R, K9, K2tog.

Row 4: SSK, K9, M1L, K2, M1R, K9, K2tog.

Row 6: SSK, K9, M1L, K2, M1R, K9, K2tog.

Row 8: SSK, K9, M1L, K2, M1R, K9, K2tog.

Rows 9–19: Work 11 rows of plain stockinette stitch, slipping the first st of every row.

Row 20: Slip 1, M1R, K8, SSK, K2, K2tog, K8, M1L, K1.

Row 22: Slip 1, M1R, K8, SSK, K2, K2tog, K8, M1L, K1.

Row 24: Slip 1, M1R, K8, SSK, K2, K2tog, K8, M1L, K1.

Row 26: Slip 1, M1R, K8, SSK, K2, K2tog, K8, M1L, K1.

• Back Left Leg

The first part of the back legs is worked flat; then it switches to knitting in the round.

Row 1: Slip 1, K9, place next 14 sts on scrap yarn, turn work. (10 sts)

Row 2: Slip 1, P1, w&t.

Row 3: K2, turn work.

Row 4: Slip 1, P3, w&t.

Row 5: K4, turn work.

Row 6: Slip 1, P5, w&t.

Row 7: K6.

Arrange sts on 3 dpns; join in the round.

Rnd 8: K2tog, K6, SSK. (8 sts)

Rnd 9: K all sts.

Rnd 10: K2tog, K4, SSK. (6 sts)

Rnd 11: K all sts.

Rnd 12: K2, (M1, K1) 2 times, K2. (8 sts)

Rnds 13–16: K all sts.

Cut yarn, thread through remaining live sts, and pull closed. Weave in loose end.

• Back Right Leg

Place last 10 sts on scrap yarn onto a dpn; leave center 4 sts on scrap yarn. With RS facing, rejoin working yarn at first st. Rows 1–7 are worked flat.

Row 1: K2, w&t.

Row 2: P2, turn work.

Row 3: Slip 1, K3, w&t.

Row 4: P4, turn work.

Row 5: Slip 1, K5, w&t.

Row 6: P6, turn work.

Row 7: Slip 1, K9.

Arrange sts on 3 dpns; join sts in the round.

Rnd 8: K2tog, K6, SSK. (8 sts)

Rnd 9: K all sts.

Rnd 10: K2tog, K4, SSK. (6 sts)

Rnd 11: K all sts.

Rnd 12: K4, (M1, K1) 2 times. (8 sts)

Rnds 13–16: K all sts.

Cut yarn, thread through remaining live sts, and pull closed. Weave in loose end.

Small triangles are now created to fit inside the inner thighs of the back legs. Work both the same. With color B, CO 6 sts onto 1 dpn and work flat.

Row 1: Slip 1, P5.

Row 2: SSK, K2, K2tog. (4 sts)

Row 3: Slip 1, P3.

Row 4: SSK, K2tog. (2 sts)

Row 5: Slip 1, P1.

Row 6: K2tog. (1 st)

Cut yarn and pull through last st. Fit inside of back legs like a puzzle piece with the CO edge even with the top of the leg and knit side facing outward; seam in place.

• Belly Piece

Place 4 color B sts from scrap yarn onto 1 dpn. The belly piece is worked flat.

Row 1 and all odd rows through 29 are worked: Slip 1, P to end.

Row 2: Slip 1, K3.

Row 4: Slip 1, M1R, K2, M1L, K1. (6 sts)

Row 6: Slip 1, K5.

Row 8: Slip 1, M1R, K4, M1L, K1. (8 sts)

Rows 9–25: Work 17 rows of plain stockinette st, slipping first st of every row.

Row 26: SSK, K4, K2tog. (6 sts)

Row 28: Slip 1, K5.

Cast off. Pin cast-off edge to the 4 live sts on scrap yarn (a dpn can also be used to secure in place). With color B, begin at the front, and seam belly piece to body on both sides. The cast-off edge should just reach the 4 sts on scrap yarn at the end of the body. Do not seam the end closed. Do not stuff body now; it's easier to knit the tail if body is left unstuffed.

• Tail

Setup: Place 4 sts from scrap yarn onto 1 dpn. With RS facing and with a 2nd dpn, begin in the center of the belly piece and PU 4 sts along the edge of work up to first live st on scrap yarn; K4. With a 3rd dpn, PU 4 sts along the opposite side of the opening down to where you started (12 sts); EOR.

Rnds 1–5: K all sts.

Rnd 6: K2, w&t.

Rnd 7: P4, w&t.

Rnd 8: K5, w&t.

Rnd 9: P6, w&t.

Rnd 10: K7, w&t.

Rnd 11: P8, w&t.

Rnd 12: K4 (EOR).

Rnd 13: K all sts.

Rnd 14: (M1, K3) 4 times. (16 sts)

Rnds 15–18: K all sts.

Rnd 19: (M1, K4) 4 times. (20 sts)

Rnds 20–39: K all sts.

Rnd 40: (M1, K5) 4 times. (24 sts)

Rnd 41: K all sts.

Rnd 42: K14, w&t.

Rnd 43: P4, w&t.

Rnd 44: K6, w&t.

Rnd 45: P8, w&t.

Rnd 46: K10, w&t.

Rnd 47: P12, w&t.

Rnd 48: K14, w&t.

Rnd 49: P16, w&t.

Rnd 50: K18, w&t.

Row 11: Slip 1, P13; with another dpn, PUP 4 sts along edge of work. (18 sts)

All sts can be placed on 1 dpn while you work the next few rows.

Row 12: Slip 1, K5, SSK, K2, K2tog, K6. (16 sts)
Row 13: Slip 1, P15.
Row 14: Slip 1, K4, SSK, K2, K2tog, K5. (14 sts)
Row 15: Slip 1, P13.
Row 16: Slip 1, K3, SSK, K2, K2tog, K4. (12 sts)

Arrange sts on 3 dpns and join in the round to work the end of the head.

Rnd 17: K all sts.
Rnd 18: K3, SSK, K2, K2tog, K3. (10 sts)
Rnd 19: K all sts.
Rnd 20: K2, SSK, K2, K2tog, K2. (8 sts)
Rnd 21: K2, SSK, K2tog, K2. (6 sts)

Cut yarn, thread through remaining live sts, and pull closed. Add safety eyes 4 rows up from neckline and 4 rows apart from each other at the top. Embroider around eyes with scrap of light-brown yarn.

Stuff head fully and seam to neck opening with back of head at back of neck opening. This will bring the nose forward past the opening.

• Ears

The ears are worked flat and seamed to head. With color A, CO 4 sts onto 1 dpn.

Row 1: P4.
Row 2: K4.
Row 3: P4.
Row 4: SSK, K2tog. (2 sts)
Row 5: P2.
Row 6: K2tog. (1 st)

Cut yarn, and pull through last st. Brush top half of ear lightly on both sides with wire brush. Seam to sides of head about 3 rows behind the eyes and 7 rows from neckline in the back. Feet are left unstuffed, flattened, and bent forward.

Rnd 51: P20, w&t.
Rnd 52: K22 (EOR).
Rnd 53: K all sts.
Rnd 54: (K2tog, K2) 6 times. (18 sts)
Rnds 55–56: K all sts.

Stuff tail now before closing.

Rnd 57: (K2tog, K1) 6 times. (12 sts)
Rnds 58–59: K all sts.
Rnd 60: (K2tog) 6 times. (6 sts)
Rnd 61: K all sts.

Cut yarn, thread through remaining live sts, and pull closed. Brush tail with wire brush. Bend tail up and over body and make a stitch where it meets the body to hold it in place. Stuff body and legs.

• Head

The first part of the head is worked flat. Work begins with the curve at back of head. With color A, CO 10 sts to 1 dpn.

Row 1: P all sts.
Row 2: K7, w&t.
Row 3: P4, w&t.
Row 4: K5, w&t.
Row 5: P6, w&t.
Row 6: K7, w&t.
Row 7: P8, w&t.
Row 8: K9 (EOR).
Row 9: Slip 1, P9.
Row 10: Slip 1, K9; with another dpn, PU 4 sts along edge of work. (14 sts)

MALLARD DUCK

✗ Sighted at Victoria Park
Kitchener, Ontario
Canada

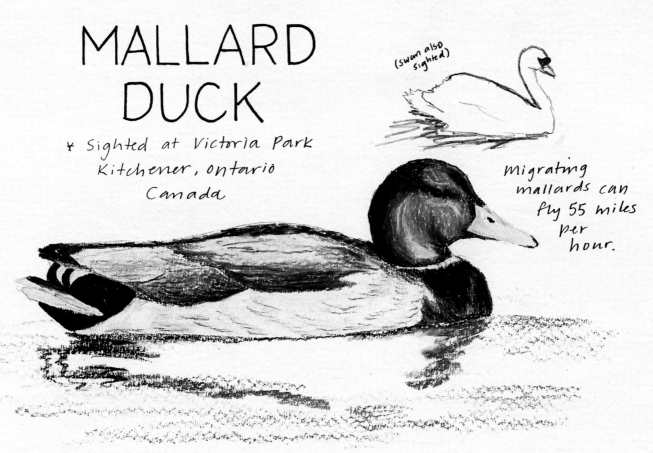

(swan also sighted)

migrating
mallards can
fly 55 miles
per
hour.

They mostly feed off of the surface of the
water, eating seeds, small fish, insects, frogs, and fish eggs.

Females call their
baby ducklings
who can hear it
for miles.

♥

Bright colored bills
suggest that a duck has
been eating right and has a strong
immune system, making them
attractive mates.

Mallard Duck

SIZE

14"/35.5 cm bill to tail feathers
6"/15 cm wide

YARN

Cascade 220, #4 medium weight, 100%
Peruvian Highland wool, 220 yd./200 m per
3.5 oz./100 g skein
Note: All colors held double in this pattern.
- A: 8505 White (body); 160 yd./146 m
- B: 2431 Chocolate Heather (breast);
  80 yd./73 m
- C: 8267 Forest Green (neck and head);
  50 yd./45.5 m
- D: 7827 Goldenrod (bill, legs, and feet);
  30 yd./27.5 m
- E: 4002 Jet (tail feathers); 20 yd./18 m
- F: 2442 Fog Hatt (wings); 100 yd./91 m

NEEDLES

US size 6/4.0 mm dpns

NOTIONS

10 mm brown safety eyes
Darning needle
Stuffing
Styrofoam (optional)
Wire or other support for legs (optional)

INSTRUCTIONS

• Body

Work begins at the top/center of a vertical line
between breast and body. With color A (held
double), CO 43 sts onto 3 dpns. Join in the round
by slipping the first CO st onto the 3rd needle
and then pulling the 2nd stitch (formerly the last
st) over it and off the needle; 42 sts remain.
Rnd 1: K all sts.
Rnd 2: K3, (M1, K6) 2 times, M1, K12, (M1, K6) 2
   times, M1, K3. (48 sts)
Rnds 3-4: K all sts.
Rnd 5: K4, (M1, K8) 5 times, M1, K4. (54 sts)
Rnds 6-7: K all sts.
Rnd 8: K5, (M1, K10) 2 times, M1, K4, (M1, K10) 2
   times, M1, K5. (60 sts)

Rnds 9-18: K all sts.
Rnd 19: K10, SSK, K6, K2tog, K20, SSK, K6, K2tog,
   K10. (56 sts)
Rnds 20-23: K all sts.
Rnd 24: K9, SSK, K6, K2tog, K18, SSK, K6, K2tog, K9.
   (52 sts)
Rnds 25-28: K all sts.
Rnd 29: K8, SSK, K6, K2tog, K16, SSK, K6, K2tog, K8.
   (48 sts)
Rnds 30-33: K all sts.
Rnd 34: K7, SSK, K6, K2tog, K14, SSK, K6, K2tog, K7.
   (44 sts)
Rnds 35-38: K all sts.
Rnd 39: K6, SSK, K6, K2tog, K12, SSK, K6, K2tog, K6.
   (40 sts)
Rnds 40-43: K all sts.
Rnd 44: K5, SSK, K6, K2tog, K10, SSK, K6, K2tog, K5.
   (36 sts)
Rnd 45: K all sts.
Rnd 46: K2, (K2, K2tog) 3 times, K8, (SSK, K2) 3
   times, K2. (30 sts)
Rnd 47: K all sts.
Rnd 48: K2, (K1, K2tog) 3 times, K8, (SSK, K1) 3
   times, K2. (24 sts)
Rnd 49: K all sts.
Rnd 50: K2, (K2tog) 3 times, K8, (SSK) 3 times, K2.
   (18 sts)
Rnd 51: K all sts.
Rnd 52: (K2tog) 3 times, K6, (SSK) 3 times. (12 sts)
Rnd 53: K all sts.
Rnd 54: K1, (K2tog) 2 times, K2, (SSK) 2 times, K1.
   (8 sts)
Rnd 55: K all sts.
   Cut yarn, thread through remaining live sts,
and pull closed. Weave in loose end. Do not stuff
body yet; it's easier to knit the breast if it is left
unstuffed.

• Breast

Sts are now picked up in the original CO sts to begin your duck's breast. With 3 dpns and RS facing, begin at the first CO st at top/center and PU 42 sts with color B (held double); join in the round. The breast is worked in short rows.

Row 1: K26, w&t.
Row 2: P10, w&t.
Row 3: K11, w&t.
Row 4: P12, w&t.
Row 5: K13, w&t.
Row 6: P14, w&t.
Row 7: K15, w&t.
Row 8: P16, w&t.
Row 9: K17, w&t.
Row 10: P18, w&t.
Row 11: K19, w&t.
Row 12: P20, w&t.
Row 13: K21, w&t.
Row 14: P22, w&t.
Row 15: K23, w&t.
Row 16: P24, w&t.
Row 17: K25, w&t.
Row 18: P26, w&t.
Row 19: K27, w&t.
Row 20: P28, w&t.
Row 21: K15, K2tog, K12, w&t. (41 sts)
Row 22: P15, P2tog, P12, w&t. (40 sts)
Row 23: K15, K2tog, K12, w&t. (39 sts)
Row 24: P15, P2tog, P12, w&t. (38 sts)

Row 25: K15, K2tog, K12, w&t. (37 sts)
Row 26: P15, P2tog, P12, w&t. (36 sts)
Row 27: K15, (K2tog) 2 times, K10, w&t. (34 sts)
Row 28: P14, (P2tog) 2 times, P10, w&t. (32 sts)
Row 29: K14, (K2tog) 2 times, K9, w&t. (30 sts)
Row 30: P13, (P2tog) 2 times, P9, w&t. (28 sts)
Row 31: K13, (K2tog) 2 times, K8, w&t. (26 sts)
Row 32: P12, (P2tog) 2 times, P8, w&t. (24 sts)
Row 33: K23 (EOR).

Cut yarn. Stuff body and breast fully except for the last 5–6 rows of the tail, which are left unstuffed and flattened. The body of the duck should not be round; after stuffing, flatten top to bottom so that the width of the body is nearly double the height.

• Neck and Head

Continue working up from the chest to shape the neck and head. Rounds 1 and 2 are worked with color A held double; switch to color C (held double) for the remainder.

Rnds 1–2: K all sts (color A). (24 sts)
Rnd 3: K all sts (color C).
Rnd 4: K9, SSK, K2, K2tog, K9. (22 sts)
Rnd 5: K all sts.
Rnd 6: K8, SSK, K2, K2tog, K8. (20 sts)
Rnd 7: K all sts.
Rnd 8: K7, SSK, K2, K2tog, K7. (18 sts)
Row 9: K2, M1, K2, w&t. (19 sts)
Row 10: P7, M1P, P2, w&t. (20 sts)

Row 11: K7, M1, K4, w&t. (21 sts)
Row 12: P9, M1P, P4, w&t. (22 sts)
Row 13: K7 (EOR).
Rnd 14: (K2, M1) 3 times, K2, SSK, K2, K2tog, K2, (M1, K2) 3 times. (26 sts)
Rnd 15: K10, SSK, K2, K2tog, K10. (24 sts)
Rnd 16: (K2, M1) 4 times, K1, SSK, K2, K2tog, K1, (M1, K2) 4 times. (30 sts)
Rnd 17: K12, SSK, K2, K2tog, K12. (28 sts)
Row 18: K4, w&t.
Row 19: P8, w&t.
Row 20: K9, w&t.
Row 21: P10, w&t.
Row 22: K11, w&t.
Row 23: P12, w&t.
Row 24: K13, w&t.
Row 25: P14, w&t.
Row 26: K7 (EOR).
Rnd 27: K11, SSK, K2, K2tog, K11. (26 sts)
Rnd 28: K10, SSK, K2, K2tog, K10. (24 sts)
Rnd 29: K9, SSK, K2, K2tog, K9. (22 sts)
Row 30: K4, w&t.
Row 31: P8, w&t.
Row 32: K9, w&t.
Row 33: P10, w&t.
Row 34: K11, w&t.
Row 35: P12, w&t.
Row 36: K13, w&t.
Row 37: P14, w&t.
Row 38: K7 (EOR).
Rnd 39: K1, (K2tog) 2 times, K11, (SSK) 2 times, K1. (18 sts)
Rnd 40: K1, (K2tog) 2 times, K7, (SSK) 2 times, K1. (14 sts)
Rnd 41: K all sts.
Rnd 42: K1, K2tog, K8, SSK, K1. (12 sts)
Rnd 43: K all sts.

Cut color C. Add more stuffing if needed to the body or breast, and stuff neck.

Leave head unstuffed for now to make knitting the bill easier. Add safety eyes about 1"/2.5 cm from color C edge and 1"/2.5 cm apart from each other on top.

• Bill

Join color D (held double).
Rnds 1–5: K all sts.
Rnd 6: K4, SSK, K2tog, K4. (10 sts)
Rnds 7–11: K all sts.
Rnd 12: K3, SSK, K2tog, K3. (8 sts)
Rnds 13–15: K all sts.

Stuff head fully, adding extra stuffing to and rounding out the "cheeks." The bill is not stuffed.

Cut color D, thread through remaining live sts, and pull closed. With color D, embroider a small bump at top/center of bill that extends into the color C section. Embroider a small black line for the nostril on each side of this. Entire bill is flattened below the nostrils.

The head beneath the eyes is brought closer together with a strand of color C: Thread a darning needle with a piece of color C, and pass it back and forth inside the head near the eyes and out the other side several times. Pull to tighten; weave in loose ends.

• Tail Feathers

The tail feathers are worked separately and seamed to the top/center of the color A end of body. They begin with a small piece worked back and forth on 2 dpns, ending with 3 small "feathers," which will naturally curl upward. With color E (held double), CO 12 sts onto 1 dpn, leaving a tail of about 12 inches for seaming.
Row 1: P all sts.
Row 2: K all sts.
Row 3: P all sts.
Row 4: SSK, K8, K2tog. (10 sts)
Row 5: P all sts.
Row 6: K all sts.
Row 7: P all sts.

Row 8: SSK, K6, K2tog. (8 sts)
Row 9: P all sts.
Row 10: K all sts.
Row 11: P all sts.
Row 12: SSK, K4, K2tog. (6 sts)
Row 13: P all sts.

The remaining 6 sts are now worked (2 at a time) to form the tail feathers.

Row 14: (K2, turn work, P2, turn work) repeat 2 times.

Cut yarn, thread through the 2 sts, pull closed, and weave in loose end. Rejoin color E at next st, and repeat row 14 two more times on remaining 4 sts. There will be a total of 3 curled tail feathers, each about 1"/2.5 cm long.

Position the flat section (purl side down) to the back of your duck so that the curled feathers are just hanging over the end of the body. Seam on all sides with the CO tail.

• Wings (make 2 the same)

The wings are worked separately, in the round, and seamed to the body. With color F held double, CO 7 sts onto 3 dpns. Join in the round by slipping the first CO st onto the 3rd needle and then pulling the 2nd stitch (formerly the last st) over it and off the needle; 6 sts remain.

Rnd 1: K all sts.
Rnd 2: M1, K to last st in round, M1, K1. (8 sts)

Repeat these two rounds until there are a total of 44 sts. K all sts for 10 rounds, and then work the following:

Row 1: K25, w&t.
Row 2: P6, w&t.
Row 3: K9, w&t.
Row 4: P12, w&t.
Row 5: K15, w&t.
Row 6: P18, w&t.
Row 7: K21, w&t.
Row 8: P24, w&t.
Row 9: K34 (EOR).
Rnd 10: (K2, K2tog) 11 times. (33 sts)
Rnd 11: K all sts.
Rnd 12: (K1, K2tog) 11 times. (22 sts)
Rnd 13: K all sts.

Arrange sts evenly on 2 dpns and close with the Kitchener stitch. Position that end on the vertical line where body and breast (colors A and B) meet. Seam to body across the front and about ⅓ of the way down each side. Additionally, tack to body about 1"/2.5 cm from end.

• Legs and Feet (make 2 the same)

With color D (held double), CO 4 sts onto 1 dpn and work 12 rows of a 4-st I-cord; then work the rows below. Rows 1–3 are worked as an I-cord (pull working yarn up from bottom st); rows 4–10 are worked flat (turn work after each row).

Row 1: (Kfb) 4 times. (8 sts)
Row 2: K8.
Row 3: K8.
Row 4: P8.
Row 5: K1, M1, K6, M1, K1. (10 sts)
Row 6: P10.
Row 7: K10.
Row 8: P10.
Row 9: K10.

Cast off all sts.

Cut yarn, leaving a tail of 1 yard, pull through last st. The tail is used to create three "toes" on each foot. The outer 2 toes are created by wrapping the 2 edge sts on each side of the feet several times, from the leg down to the cast-off edge, starting wider and ending up more narrow. The center toe is created the same way, by wrapping 2 sts straight down the center of the foot from the leg to the cast-off edge. Once finished, the toes can be further defined by embroidering between them with color B.

In order for your duck to stand on its legs and feet, a straight stick, dpn, or heavy wire will need to be inserted from the bottom up through the I-cord leg and into the body. The other end (below the foot) can be stuck into a block of Styrofoam or any firm base.

BLACK-TAILED JACKRABBIT

It is not really a rabbit, but a hare - because its young are born with fur and with their eyes open.

* Sighted off the El camino del Diablo Hwy Yuma County, Arizona

They are found from Baja California and South-Central Mexico to West-Central and Western United States

The black-tailed jackrabbits most identifying feature is its huge ears which help to cool body temperature. They are tipped with black fur.

Black-tailed Jackrabbits have large eyes that are placed high on their head and nearer to the sides, enabling them to see almost 360° and helping them to spot predators.

Long, powerful rear legs

Black-Tailed Jackrabbit

SIZE

12"/30.5 cm top of ears to bottom of feet
5"/12.5 cm wide

YARN

Cascade Aereo, #4 medium weight, 47% merino wool/31% baby alpaca/22% nylon, 240 yd./220 m per 3.5 oz./100 g skein

- A suggestions: 05 Doeskin Heather; 06 Walnut Heather (body, head, legs, ears); 120 yd./110 m
- B: 07 Mocha Heather (nose); 1 yd./1 m
- C: 04 Ecru (embroidery around eyes); 1 yd./1 m
- D: 01 Jet (tips of ears; tail); 10 yd./9 m

NEEDLES

US size 5/3.75 mm dpns

NOTIONS

12 mm brown safety eyes
Darning needle
Medium-weight hobby wire (to hold up ears; optional)
Stitch marker
Stuffing
White sewing thread (whiskers; optional)

INSTRUCTIONS

• Chest

Work begins at neckline. Chest is worked flat; turn work after each row. With color A, CO 20 sts onto 1 dpn.
Row 1: P all sts.
Row 2: K all sts.
Row 3: P all sts.
Row 4: K all sts.
Row 5: P all sts.
Row 6: K1, M1R, K18, M1L, K1. (22 sts)
Row 7: P all sts.
Row 8: K all sts.
Row 9: P all sts.
Row 10: K1, M1R, K20, M1L, K1. (24 sts)
Row 11: P all sts.
Row 12: K all sts.
Row 13: P all sts.
Row 14: K all sts.

Row 15: P all sts.
Row 16: K all sts.
Row 17: P all sts.
Row 18: K all sts.
Row 19: P all sts.
Row 20: K16, w&t.
Row 21: P8, w&t.
Row 22: K10, w&t.
Row 23: P12, w&t.
Row 24: K14, w&t.
Row 25: P16, w&t.
Row 26: K18, w&t.
Row 27: P20, w&t.
Row 28: K22 (EOR).

• Front Left Leg and Paw

Arrange last 12 sts worked on 3 dpns; join in the round. Place first 12 sts onto a piece of scrap yarn.
Rnds 1–3: K all sts.

The "elbow" is now shaped using some of the sts. K2 and then arrange sts 3–8 on 1 dpn and sts 9–12 plus 1 and 2 on a 2nd dpn. The rows below are worked over sts 9–2 at back of leg. Turn work after each one:
Row 1: Slip 1, P5.
Row 2: Slip 1, K5.
Row 3: Slip 1, P5.
Row 4: Slip 1, K5.

Arrange these 6 sts on 2 dpns (3–3) and hold with right sides facing each other; work a 3-needle bind-off. Cut yarn; pull through last st. Turn work right-side out. Rejoin working yarn at first st on needle; K6. With a 2nd needle, PU 4 sts along the top edge of the elbow from live sts on 1st needle to bind off seam (EOR). With a 3rd needle, PU 4 sts along the opposite edge; K10 (EOR). 14 sts total.
Rnd 1: K all sts.
Rnd 2: K2tog, K10, SSK. (12 sts)
Rnd 3: K all sts.
Rnd 4: K2tog, K8, SSK. (10 sts)
Rnd 5: K all sts.
Rnd 6: K2tog, K6, SSK. (8 sts)
Rnds 7–24: K all sts.
Rnd 25: K3, M1L, K2, M1R, K3. (10 sts)
Rnds 26–29: K all sts.

Cut yarn, thread through remaining live sts, and pull closed. Stuff leg and paw loosely to keep them thin. When standing, last 2–3 rows of paw will be bent to lay flat on surface.

• Front Right Leg and Paw

Place live sts from scrap yarn onto 3 dpns. With RS facing, rejoin working yarn at first st; K12. Join sts in the round; K 2 rounds.

K4, and then arrange sts 1–4 plus 11 and 12 on 1 dpn, and sts 5–10 on a 2nd dpn. The elbow is shaped with sts 1–4 plus 11 and 12.

Repeat all remaining instructions the same as the left leg.

• Body

Setup: Seam top 3 rows of chest together in the back, forming a circle for the neck. Sts are now picked up along the edge of chest to create the body. A total of 40 sts are picked up with 3 dpns as follows:

- 1st dpn: PU 16 sts from top/center neck seam to right leg elbow
- 2nd dpn: PU 8 sts from right leg elbow to left leg elbow
- 3rd dpn: PU 16 sts from left leg elbow to top/center neck seam

These sts can be rearranged on needles as you work.

The back is shaped with sets of short rows alternated with either plain knit rounds or increase rounds. All of the short row sets are worked the same. Refer to these instructions every time short rows are indicated, and work all rows 1–9 every time:

SHORT ROWS

Row 1: K4, w&t.
Row 2: P8, w&t.
Row 3: K12, w&t.
Row 4: P16, w&t.
Row 5: K20, w&t.
Row 6: P24, w&t.
Row 7: K28, w&t.
Row 8: P32, w&t.
Row 9: K16 (EOR).

Rnds 1–2: K all sts.
  Work short rows.
Rnds 3–4: K all sts.
  Work short rows.
Rnds 5–6: K all sts.
  Work short rows.
Rnd 7: K6, M1, K28, M1, K6. (42 sts)
Rnd 8: K all sts.
  Work short rows.
Rnd 9: K6, M1, K30, M1, K6. (44 sts)
Rnd 10: K all sts.
  Work short rows.
Rnd 11: K6, M1, K32, M1, K6. (46 sts)
Rnds 12–14: K all sts.
Rnd 15: (K1, K2tog, K17, SSK, K1) 2 times. (42 sts)
Rnd 16: K all sts.
Rnd 17: (K1, K2tog, K15, SSK, K1) 2 times. (38 sts)
Rnd 18: K all sts.
Rnd 19: (K1, K2tog, K13, SSK, K1) 2 times. (34 sts)
Rnd 20: K all sts.

Rnd 21: (K1, K2tog K11, SSK, K1) 2 times. (30 sts)
Rnd 22: K all sts.
Rnd 23: (K1, K2tog, K9, SSK, K1) 2 times. (26 sts)
Rnd 24: K all sts.
Rnd 25: (K1, K2tog, K7, SSK, K1) 2 times. (22 sts)
Rnd 26: K all sts.
Rnd 27: (K1, K2tog, K5, SSK, K1) 2 times. (18 sts)
Rnds 28-30: K all sts.

Cut yarn, thread through remaining live sts, and pull closed. Weave in loose ends. Stuff body and front legs.

• Back Legs and Feet (make 2 the same)

The back legs and feet are worked separate from the body and all in one piece. It begins with the bend in the front of the leg, which then separates into 2 parts. CO 12 sts onto 1 dpn; the first part is worked flat.

Row 1: P all sts.
Row 2: K all sts.
Row 3: P all sts.
Row 4: K8, w&t.
Row 5: P4, w&t.
Row 6: K5, w&t.
Row 7: P6, w&t.
Row 8: K7, w&t.
Row 9: P8, w&t.
Row 10: K9, w&t.
Row 11: P10, w&t.
Row 12: K11 (EOR).
Row 13: P all sts.
Row 14: K all sts.

Arrange sts on 2 dpns (6-6). With RS facing, PU a total of 12 sts around the edge of your work—2 on each side, and 8 along the CO edge. It's best to use 2 additional dpns for this step (total of 4 plus 1 working dpn); 24 sts (EOR). Join sts in the round.
Rnd 15: K all sts.
Setup: K6; place next 12 sts on scrap yarn. Arrange first and last 6 sts on 3 dpns (maintaining same EOR); join in the round. K6 (EOR). (12 sts)
Rnds 16-18: K all sts.
Rnd 19: K4, SSK, K2tog, K4. (10 sts)
Rnds 20-25: K all sts.
Rnd 26: K3, SSK, K2tog, K3. (8 sts)
Rnds 27-33: K all sts.

The "heel" is worked like the elbows. K2, and then arrange sts 2-7 on 1 dpn, and st 8 plus st 1 on a 2nd dpn. The rows below are worked over sts 2-7, turning your work after each one.

Row 1: Slip 1, K5.
Row 2: Slip 1, P5.
Row 3: Slip 1, K5.
Row 4: Slip 1, P5.

Arrange these 6 sts on 2 dpns (3-3) and hold right sides facing each other. Work a 3-needle bind-off. Cut yarn and pull through last st. Turn work right-side out. With RS facing, rejoin working yarn at first st on needle; K2.

With a 2nd needle, PU 4 sts along the top edge of the heel from live sts on 1st needle to bind off seam (EOR). With a 3rd needle, PU 4 sts along the opposite edge; K6 (EOR). (10 sts)
Rnds 1-2: K all sts.
Rnd 3: K4, M1L, K2, M1R, K4. (12 sts)
Rnds 4-8: K all sts.
Rnd 9: K5, M1L, K2, M1R, K5. (14 sts)
Rnds 10-12: K all sts.
Row 13: K8, w&t.
Row 14: P2, w&t.
Row 15: K3, w&t.
Row 16: P4, w&t.
Row 17: K9 (EOR).
Rnd 18: K all sts.
Rnd 19: (K2tog) 2 times, K6, (SSK) 2 times. (10 sts)
Rnd 20: K all sts.
Rnd 21: K2tog, K6, SSK. (8 sts)

Cut yarn, thread through remaining live sts, and pull closed. Stuff through opening at top, using a dpn from the outside to shift stuffing evenly around and accentuate the heel.
Setup for second part of leg: Place 12 sts from scrap yarn onto 2 dpns (6-6). With RS facing, rejoin working yarn at 7th st; K6. With a 3rd dpn, PU 4 sts below the 12 live sts, K6 (16 sts); EOR.
Rnds 1-3: K all sts.
Rnd 4: (M1, K4) 4 times. (20 sts)
Rnds 5-16: K all sts.
Rnd 17: K2tog, K16, SSK. (18 sts)
Rnd 18: K all sts.
Rnd 19: K2tog, K14, SSK. (16 sts)
Rnd 20: K all sts.
Rnd 21: K2tog, K12, SSK. (14 sts)
Rnd 22: K all sts.
Rnd 23: K2tog, K10, SSK. (12 sts)
Rnds 24-25: K all sts.

Stuff lightly. Cut yarn, thread through remaining live sts, and pull closed.

After knitting both legs, hold them in place against the body, checking from all sides to make sure their positioning mirrors each other. Hold to

body and secure in place with a dpn (if desired); then seam to body from the topmost point on the leg around the back to the bottommost point; the front of the leg will remain open and is not seamed.

• Head

The head is worked separately and seamed to the neck when completed. Work begins at the snout and is worked flat at first; then it switches to in-the-round knitting. CO 6 sts onto 1 dpn.
Row 1: P all sts.
Row 2: K all sts.
Row 3: P all sts.
Row 4: K4, w&t.
Row 5: P2, w&t.
Row 6: K3, w&t.
Row 7: P4, w&t.
Row 8: K5 (EOR).
Row 9: P all sts.

Row 10: K all sts.
Setup: Arrange sts on 2 dpns (3–3). With RS facing and 2 more dpns, PU 6 more sts around the edges of your work, 1 along each side, and 4 on the CO edge; K3. This is the center/bottom of the snout and the EOR (12 sts). It's important to use a st marker or something else here; it's easy to lose track of it while knitting the head. Join sts in the round.
Rnd 11: K all sts.
Rnd 12: K5, M1L, K2, M1R, K5. (14 sts)
Rnd 13: K all sts.
Rnd 14: K6, M1L, K2, M1R, K6. (16 sts)
Rnds 15–16: K all sts.
Rnd 17: K1, (M1L, K2) 4 times, (M1R, K2) 3 times, M1R, K1. (24 sts)
Rnds 18–23: K all sts.
Rnd 24: K11, M1L, K2, M1R, K11. (26 sts)
Rnds 25–27: K all sts.

Rnd 28: K7, cast off next 4 sts, K3, cast off next 4 sts, K6. (18 sts)

Note: There should be 4 knit sts at top of head with 4 cast-off sts on each side. These will be the holes for the ears.

Rnd 29: K7, CO 4 sts, K4, CO 4 sts, K7. (26 sts)

Rnds 30–32: K all sts.

Arrange all sts on 2 dpns: 1–13 on one and 14–26 on the other; close with the Kitchener stitch.

• Finishing Details on Head

Insert safety eyes through ear holes. They should be placed about 3 sts down from the ear holes and about 1"/2.5 cm apart from each other.

Embroider a line around the eye with color C.

Stuff head through ear holes.

Embroider nose with color B as a triangle with point downward.

With color B, embroider a ½"/1.25 cm line down from nose, inserting needle back up at the beginning of line, and pull tightly, creating a small rounding on either side.

Whiskers can be added with white sewing thread.

• Ears (make 2 the same)

Sts are now picked up around the openings at top of head to work the ears. With RS facing, begin in the center/front of opening and PU 12 sts with 3 dpns, leaving a tail of a few inches. Join sts in the round and work the first 7 rounds below; then switch to flat knitting for the remainder of the ear. Sts can be arranged all on one dpn after a few rows.

Rnds 1–7: K all sts.

Row 8: Slip 1, P11.

Row 9: Slip 1, K11.

Row 10: Slip 1, P11.

Row 11: Slip 1, K11.

Row 12: Slip 1, P11.

Row 13: Slip 1, M1L, K10, M1R, K1. (14 sts)

Rows 14–28: Continue working in stockinette stitch, slipping the first st of each row.

Row 29: (SSK) 2 times, K6, (K2tog) 2 times. (10 sts)

Row 30: Slip 1, P9.

Row 31: (SSK) 2 times, K2, (K2tog) 2 times. (6 sts)

Row 32: Slip 1, P5.

Row 33: Slip 1, cast off remaining sts.

Cut yarn and pull through last st. Do not weave in loose ends at this point. The ears will naturally curve inward, just like real rabbits' ears do.

If your jackrabbit is to be given to a child to play with and love, then I recommend seaming the ears together at the bottom to help them stand up as much as possible. If your rabbit will sit on a shelf, I recommend using a medium-weight hobby wire to maintain proper jackrabbit ear position. Cut a piece about 12 inches long and fold in half. Fold up about 2 inches of the closed end, creating about a 2-inch base with 4 strands of wire. This is the side that will go down inside the head. Separate the two pieces of the top half slightly, about the width of the ear. Lay each piece inside the roll of fabric on each side of the ear. With the loose ends of yarn, subtly sew around the wire on each side of the ear to help hold it in place and keep it from showing.

With color D, embroider with whipstitch around the tips of the ears, about 1"/2.5 cm on each side of the center. Leave a tail with color D also so that it can be used to wrap around the wire at the top of the ear, the same as the sides.

Make sure the neck is stuffed fully. Place head into desired position (rabbit can be looking in any direction) with back of head even with neck stitches; seam in place.

• Tail

The tail is worked flat with the intarsia method of colorwork and seamed to your rabbit afterward. Begin by preparing a very small ball of color A (2–3 yards). CO a total of 12 sts to 1 dpn in the following colors and amounts:

- Color A: CO 4 sts
- Color D: CO 4 sts
- Color A: CO 4 sts

When working intarsia, always bring the new color over the old one to prevent a gap from forming between them. This is true whether you are knitting the sts on the right side of the work or purling them on the wrong side.

Row 1: Color A: P4; Color D: P4; Color A: P4.

Row 2: Color A: K4; Color D: K4; Color A: K4.

Row 3: Color A: P4; Color D: P4; Color A: P4.

Row 4: Color A: K4; Color D: K4; Color A: K4.

Row 5: Color A: P4; Color D: P4; Color A: P4.

Row 6: Color A: K4; Color B: K4; Color A: K4.

Row 7: Color A: P4; Color D: P4; Color A: P4.

Row 8: Color A: SSK, K2 (3 sts); Color D: K2tog, SSK (2 sts); Color A: K2, K2tog (3 sts).

Row 9: Color A: P3; Color D: P2; Color A: P3.

Row 10: Color A: SSK, K1 (2 sts); Color D: K2tog (1 st); Color A: K1, K2tog (2 sts).

Row 11: Color A: P2; Color D: P1; Color A: P2.

Cut all strands of yarn. Thread color A through remaining live sts and pull closed. Seam back closed with color A. Stuff loose ends into top of tail. Seam CO edge to bottom of rabbit with black stripe pointed up.

Flatback turtles grow to be 31 to 37 inches long and weigh 220 pounds!

The greatest threats facing flatback turtles include accidental capture by fisheries targeting other species, pollution, and collection of eggs.

Flatback turtles spend most of their time in the water with females only coming to shore to lay eggs.

After mating out at sea, females will visit a sandy beach several times during the course of the nesting season, dig a burrow, and lay approximately 50 eggs each time!

FLATBACK SEA TURTLE

* Sighted at Crab Island Cape York Peninsula Australia

Flatback Sea Turtle

SIZE

12"/30.5 cm long
11"/28 cm wide

YARN

Cascade 220, #4 medium weight, 100%
Peruvian Highland wool, 220 yd./200 m per
3.5 oz./100 g skein
- A suggestions: 8401 Silver Grey; 8021 Beige
  (head and legs); 30 yd./27.5 m
- B suggestions: 8010 Natural; 9600 Antiqued
  Heather (body and underside of shell); 120
  yd./110 m
- C suggestions: 2452 Turtle; 2425 Provence
  (carapace); 120 yd./110 m

NEEDLES

US size 3/3.25 mm dpns
US size 6/4 mm straight needles

NOTIONS

6 mm x 8 mm black oval safety eyes
Darning needle
Stuffing

INSTRUCTIONS

• Head

The head is worked in two pieces: top and
bottom. Work begins at beak on both pieces.
With color A, CO 12 sts onto 1 dpn. Rows 1–18 are
worked back and forth.
Row 1: P all sts.
Row 2: K all sts.
Row 3: P all sts.
Row 4: K7, w&t.
Row 5: P2, w&t.
Row 6: K3, w&t.
Row 7: P4, w&t.
Row 8: K5, w&t.
Row 9: P6, w&t.
Row 10: K7, w&t.
Row 11: P8, w&t.
Row 12: K9, w&t.
Row 13: P10, w&t.
Row 14: K11 (EOR).

Row 15: P all sts.
Row 16: K all sts.
Row 17: P all sts.
Row 18: K all sts.
   Arrange sts on 2 dpns. Cut yarn; set aside. With
color A, CO 12 sts onto another dpn and repeat
rows 1–15 only for the bottom piece. Then K6 (new
EOR), K6. Arrange these 12 sts on 2 dpns. Because
it is divided into 4 sections, I recommend that
you use a set of 5 dpns (4 with sts and 1 working
dpn) from now through end of body.
   The top and bottom pieces are now joined in
the round: with working yarn coming from the
last st of the bottom piece, K12 (the sts in the
top piece). Now join with the final 6 sts from
the bottom piece; K6 (EOR). K all sts for 1 round.
(24 sts)
   Leave the head open with the 2 pieces
separated for now while the body is worked.

• Body

First prepare 2 5-yard pieces of color B; set aside.
Cut color A; join color B.
Rnd 1: K all sts.
Rnd 2: P all sts.
Rnd 3: K all sts.
Rnd 4: (K5, M1L, K2, M1R, K5) 2 times. (28 sts)
Rnd 5: P all sts.
Rnd 6: K all sts.
Rnd 7: (K6, M1L, K2, M1R, K6) 2 times. (32 sts)
Rnd 8: K all sts.
Rnd 9: (K7, M1L, K2, M1R, K7) 2 times. (36 sts)
Rnd 10: K all sts.
Rnd 11: (K8, M1L, K2, M1R, K8) 2 times. (40 sts)
Rnd 12: K all sts.
Rnd 13: (K9, M1L, K2, M1R, K9) 2 times. (44 sts)

• Front Leg Openings

To shape the front leg openings, rows 15–24 are
worked back and forth on half of the sts at a
time; turn work after each one.
Row 14: K11.
Row 15: Slip 1, P21.
Row 16: Slip 1, M1R, K20, M1L, K1. (24 sts)
Row 17: Slip 1, P23.
Row 18: Slip 1, K23.
Row 19: Slip 1, P23.

Row 20: Slip 1, M1R, K22, M1L, K1. (26 sts)
Row 21: Slip 1, P25.
Row 22: Slip 1, K25.
Row 23: Slip 1, P25.
Row 24: Slip 1, K12 (EOR).

   Do not break yarn; leave sts on 2 dpns.

   With RS facing, join one of the 5-yard pieces of color B at next st in round; K22. Work rows 15–23 again; cut yarn.

   Working in the round with all of the sts is now resumed. Begin at EOR with working ball of yarn.
Rnd 25: (K12, M1L, K2, M1R, K12) 2 times. (56 sts)
Rnd 26: K all sts.
Rnd 27: (K13, M1L, K2, M1R, K13) 2 times. (60 sts)
Rnd 28: K all sts.
Rnd 29: (K14, M1L, K2, M1R, K14) 2 times. (64 sts)
Rnd 30: K all sts.
Rnd 31: (K15, M1L, K2, M1R, K15) 2 times. (68 sts)
Rnd 32: K all sts.
Rnd 33: (K16, M1L, K2, M1R, K16) 2 times. (72 sts)
Rnds 34–51: K all sts for 18 rounds.
Rnd 52: (K15, SSK, K2, K2tog, K15) 2 times. (68 sts)
Rnd 53: K all sts.
Rnd 54: (K14, SSK, K2, K2tog, K14) 2 times. (64 sts)
Rnd 55: K all sts.
Rnd 56: (K13, SSK, K2, K2tog, K13) 2 times. (60 sts)
Rnd 57: K all sts.
Rnd 58: (K12, SSK, K2, K2tog, K12) 2 times. (56 sts)
Rnd 59: K all sts.
Rnd 60: (K11, SSK, K2, K2tog, K11) 2 times. (52 sts)
Rnd 61: K all sts.

• Back Leg Openings

The back leg openings are now worked in the same way that the front legs were.
Row 62: K13.
Row 63: Slip 1, P25.
Row 64: Slip 1, K2tog, K20, SSK, K1. (24 sts)
Row 65: Slip 1, P23.
Row 66: Slip 1, K23.
Row 67: Slip 1, P23.
Row 68: Slip 1, K2tog, K18, SSK, K1. (22 sts)
Row 69: Slip 1, P21.
Row 70: Slip 1, K10 (EOR).

   Do not break yarn; leave sts on 2 dpns.

   With RS facing, join the second 5-yard piece of color B at next st in round and K26. Work rows 63–69 again; cut yarn.

   Working in the round with all of the sts is now resumed. Begin at EOR with working ball of yarn.

Rnd 71: (K8, SSK, K2, K2tog, K8) 2 times. (40 sts)
Rnd 72: K all sts.
Rnd 73: (K7, SSK, K2, K2tog, K7) 2 times. (36 sts)
Rnd 74: K all sts.
Rnd 75: (K6, SSK, K2, K2tog, K6) 2 times. (32 sts)
Rnd 76: K all sts.

   Live sts are now taken off the needles and placed on a piece of scrap yarn to be finished after working the 4 legs. Measure off about 10 yards of working yarn, cut yarn, and then roll it into a small ball and tuck it inside the body. Work all 4 legs.

• Front Legs (make 2 the same)

Sts are now picked up around the first two openings created while working the body. With the head pointed up, begin with 1 dpn only and color A, PU 3 sts at bottom of opening: 1 on the right side of center, and 2 on the left side; turn work. Rows 1–4 are worked back and forth.
Row 1: P3, PUP 1 st. (4 sts)
Row 2: K4, PU 1 st. (5 sts)
Row 3: P5, PUP 1 st. (6 sts)
Row 4: K3 (EOR).
Setup to work in the round: Arrange sts on 2 dpns to indicate EOR in the middle of them; K3. With a 3rd dpn, PU 5 sts from last st worked to top/center of opening. With a 4th dpn, PU 5 sts from top/center to last 3 sts; K3 (EOR). (16 sts)
Rnds 1–10: K all sts.

Short rows are now worked back and forth over just some of the sts to shape the bend in the arm.

Row 11: K9, w&t.
Row 12: P2, w&t.
Row 13: K3, w&t.
Row 14: P4, w&t.
Row 15: K5, w&t.
Row 16: P6, w&t.
Row 17: K7, w&t.
Row 18: P8, w&t.
Row 19: K12 (EOR).

Knitting in the round over all the sts is now resumed.

Rnd 20: K all sts.
Rnd 21: (M1, K4) 4 times. (20 sts)
Rnds 22–28: K all sts.
Rnd 29: K8, SSK, K2tog, K8. (18 sts)
Rnd 30: K all sts.
Rnd 31: K7, SSK, K2tog, K7. (16 sts)
Rnd 32: K all sts.
Rnd 33: K6, SSK, K2tog, K6. (14 sts)
Rnd 34: K all sts.
Rnd 35: K5, SSK, K2tog, K5. (12 sts)
Rnd 36: K all sts.
Rnd 37: K4, SSK, K2tog, K4. (10 sts)
Rnd 38: K all sts.

Cut yarn, thread through remaining live sts, and pull closed.

• Back Legs (make 2 the same)

Rows 1–4 are worked the same way as the front legs; however, the head is pointed down this time so that work begins at the top of the opening instead of the bottom. With head pointed down, begin with 1 dpn and color A, PU 3 sts at top of opening: 1 on the right side of center, and 2 on the left side; turn work.

Row 1: P3, PUP 1 st. (4 sts)
Row 2: K4, PU 1 st. (5 sts)
Row 3: P5, PUP 1 st. (6 sts)
Row 4: K3 (EOR).
Set up to work in the round: Arrange sts on 2 dpns to indicate EOR in the middle of them; K3. With a 3rd dpn, PU 5 sts from last st worked to bottom/center of opening. With a 4th dpn, PU 5 sts from bottom/center to last 3 sts; K3 (EOR). (16 sts)
Rnds 1–4: K all sts.
Rnd 5: (M1, K8) 2 times. (18 sts)
Rnds 6–7: K all sts.
Rnd 8: K7, SSK, K2tog, K7. (16 sts)

Rnd 9: K all sts.
Rnd 10: K6, SSK, K2tog, K6. (14 sts)
Rnd 11: K all sts.
Rnd 12: K5, SSK, K2tog, K5. (12 sts)
Rnd 13: K all sts.
Rnd 14: K4, SSK, K2tog, K4. (10 sts)

Cut yarn, thread through remaining live sts, and pull closed. Body and legs can now be stuffed using a dpn from the outside to shift stuffing around inside and make it even. Very little stuffing is added to the flipper end of the front legs; same with the back legs.

• End of Body

Place live sts from scrap yarn back onto 4 dpns and work the end of body with the reserve of color B, adding more stuffing as needed just before closing.

Rnd 1: (K5, SSK, K2, K2tog, K5) 2 times. (28 sts)
Rnd 2: K all sts.
Rnd 3: (K4, SSK, K2, K2tog, K4) 2 times. (24 sts)
Rnd 4: (K3, SSK, K2, K2tog, K3) 2 times. (20 sts)
Rnd 5: (K2, SSK, K2, K2tog, K2) 2 times. (16 sts)
Rnd 6: (K1, SSK, K2, K2tog, K1) 2 times. (12 sts)
Rnd 7: (SSK, K2, K2tog) 2 times. (8 sts)

• Carapace

The carapace is worked flat on size 6 straight needles with 4 sts of color B on each side and color C (held double) in the center. These are worked with the intarsia method of colorwork. When switching colors, always bring the new color over the old one to prevent a gap from forming between them.

Begin by preparing a second ball of color B (about 5 yards) and a second ball of color C (about 50 yards, since it is held double).

CO the following number of sts and colors to 1 straight needle:

CO 4 sts color B
CO 2 sts color C (yarn held double)
CO 4 sts color B

The carapace is worked in stockinette st and begins at the tail end.

All odd rows are purled with the same colors used in the previous K row.

Row 1: Color B: P4; Color C: P2; Color B: P4.
Row 2: Color B: K4; Color C: (Kfb) 2 times (4 sts); Color B: K4.
Row 4: Color B: K4; Color C: (Kfb) 4 times (8 sts); Color B: K4.

Row 6: Color B: K4; Color C: Kfb, K6, Kfb (10 sts); Color B: K4.

Row 8: Color B: K4; Color C: Kfb, K8, Kfb (12 sts); Color B: K4.

Row 10: Color B: K4; Color C: Kfb, K10, Kfb (14 sts); Color B: K4.

Row 12: Color B: K4; Color C: Kfb, K12, Kfb (16 sts); Color B: K4.

Row 14: Color B: K4; Color C: Kfb, K14, Kfb (18 sts); Color B: K4.

Rnd 16: Color B: K4; Color C: Kfb, K16, Kfb (20 sts); Color B: K4.

Rnd 18: Color B: K4; Color C: Kfb, K18, Kfb (22 sts); Color B: K4.

Row 20: Color B: K4; Color C: Kfb, K20, Kfb (24 sts); Color B: K4.

Row 22: Color B: K4; Color C: Kfb, K22, Kfb (26 sts); Color B: K4.

Row 24: Color B: K4; Color C: Kfb, K24, Kfb (28 sts); Color B: K4.

Row 26: Color B: K4; Color C: Kfb, K26, Kfb (30 sts); Color B: K4.

Row 28: Color B: K4; Color C: Kfb, K28, Kfb (32 sts); Color B: K4.

Work rows 29–41 in straight stockinette stitch with the st count unchanging and in the same colors as row 28, and then proceed below. Odd rows continue as before.

Row 42: Color B: K4; Color C: K2tog, K28, SSK (30 sts); Color B: K4.

Row 44: Color B: K4; Color C: K2tog, K26, SSK (28 sts); Color B: K4.

Row 46: Color B: K4; Color C: K2tog, K24, SSK (26 sts); Color B: K4.

Row 48: Color B: K4; Color C: K2tog, K22, SSK (24 sts); Color B: K4.

Row 50: Color B: K4; Color C: K2tog, K20, SSK (22 sts): Color B: K4.

Row 52: Color B: K4; Color C: K2tog, K18, SSK (20 sts); Color B: K4.

Row 54: Color B: K4; Color C: K2tog, K16, SSK (18 sts); Color B: K4.

Row 56: Color B: K4; Color C: K2tog, K14, SSK (16 sts); Color B: K4.

Row 58: Color B: K4; Color C: K2tog, K12, SSK (14 sts); Color B: K4.

Row 60: Color B: K4; Color C: K2tog, K10, SSK (12 sts); Color B: K4.

Row 62: Color B: K4; Color C: K2tog, K8, SSK (10 sts); Color B: K4.

Row 64: Cast off first 2 sts with color B. K last color B st with color C. Pull the last color B st over it and off needle. (K2tog, cast off 1) 2 times. (K1, cast off 1) 2 times. (SSK, cast off 1) 2 times. Cast off last 4 sts with color B.

Position carapace on the back of your sea turtle, and use a dpn to pin in place. The cast-off edge should be just below 2nd P row at neck, and the tail end should hang off body about ½"/1.25 cm.

With color C yarn, seam to body about ¼"/0.6 cm from the edge all around, folding the color B side under as you go. This will create the characteristic turned up edges of the Flatback.

Attach safety eyes to the head through the mouth 8 rows in front of the color B purl row and about 4 sts apart from each other on top. Embroidery with color A can be added around the eyes to make them appear deeper set. Pinch fabric at the end of the top piece and seam together with color A to form a nose. Small black dots are embroidered for the nostrils.

The top and bottom pieces of the mouth are folded under at the wrap-and-turns to shape the "lips" and then seamed together with color A. I embroidered a single strand of color A from one side of the mouth to the other and pulled it tight to accentuate where the two pieces meet and form the mouth.

BABY FLATBACK SEA TURTLE

✱ Sighted at Crab Island Cape York Peninsula, Australia

Smallest distribution of all sea turtles and that breed and nest only in Australia.

Named after its flat carapace, or shell, which is unlike the curved shell of other sea turtle species

After several weeks, the baby flatback turtles hatch, emerge from the sand, and enter the water together.

The sex of the hatchling is determined by the temperature of the sand the egg is in. If the temperature is below 84°F (29°C) the hatchling will be male. If the temperature is above, it will be female.

Hatchlings are larger than other sea turtle hatchlings, with its its. shell length averaging 2.4 in.

Baby Flatback Sea Turtle

SIZE

2.5"/6.25 cm long
3"/7.5 cm wide

YARN

Cascade 220, #4 medium weight, 100%
Peruvian Highland wool, 220 yd./200 m per
3.5 oz./100 g skein
- A: 8400 Charcoal Grey (head, legs, embroidery on carapace); 10 yd./9 m
- B: 8010 Natural (body); 10 yd./9 m
- C: 8401 Silver Grey (carapace); 5 yd./4.5 m

NEEDLES

US size 3/3.25 mm dpns

NOTIONS

6 mm x 8 mm black oval safety eyes
Darning needle
Stitch marker (optional)
Stuffing

INSTRUCTIONS

• Head

Work begins at beak. With color A, CO 5 sts onto
1 dpn. Pull yarn up from last st and work 1 row
of a 5-st I-cord. Pulling yarn up from the last st
again, (Kfb) 5 times (10 sts). Arrange sts onto 3
dpns and join in the round. Place a st marker or a
piece of scrap yarn here to mark EOR. K 3 rounds.
Cut color A; join color B.

• Body

Continue working in the round from the
preceding sts.
Rnd 1: K all sts.
Rnd 2: P all sts.
Rnd 3: K all sts.
Rnd 4: (K2, M1L, K1, M1R, K2) 2 times. (14 sts)
Rnd 5: K all sts.
Rnd 6: (K3, M1L, K1, M1R, K3) 2 times. (18 sts)
Rnds 7–12: K all sts.
Rnd 13: (K2, SSK, K1, K2tog, K2) 2 times. (14 sts)
Rnd 14: K all sts.
Rnd 15: (K1, SSK, K1, K2tog, K1) 2 times. (10 sts)

Rnd 16: K all sts.
   Cut yarn, and thread through remaining live sts.
Add a tiny bit of stuffing; pull closed. Loose ends
can be used as stuffing if preferred. Body should
be flattened with increases and decreases along
the sides. EOR is in the center/underside of baby
turtle.

• Front Legs

Left Leg: With top side facing, head pointed to
the right, and color A, PU 4 sts in a straight line
extending downward from the P round on the left
side of your baby turtle.
Rows 1–4: Work 4 rows of a 4-st I-cord.
Row 5: Turn work, P4.
Row 6: Turn work, K4.
Row 7: Turn work, P4.
Row 8: Turn work, SSK, K2tog.
   Cut yarn, thread through remaining live sts, and
pull closed. Weave in loose ends on the WS.
   Right Leg: With top side facing, head pointed
to the left, and color A, PU 4 sts in a straight line
extending upward to the P round on the right side
of your baby turtle. Repeat rows 1–8 and finishing
instructions for the left leg.

• Back Legs

Right Leg: With top side facing, head pointed to the left, and color A, PU 4 sts in a straight line extending upward one st from the end of body on the right side. Work 3 rows of a 4-st I-cord. Cut yarn, thread through live sts, and pull closed. Weave in loose end.

Left Leg: With top side facing, head pointed to the right and color A, PU 4 sts in a straight line extending downward to one st from the end of body on the left side. Work 3 rows of a 4-st I-cord. Cut yarn, thread through live sts, and pull closed. Weave in loose end.

• Carapace

Work begins at bottom of the carapace (opposite from the head) and is worked flat. With color C, CO 3 sts onto 1 dpn.

Row 1 and odd rows 3-17: P all sts.
Row 2: K1, M1R, K1, M1L, K1. (5 sts)
Row 4: K1, M1R, K3, M1L, K1. (7 sts)

Row 6: K1, M1R, K5, M1L, K1. (9 sts)
Row 8: K1, M1R, K7, M1L, K1. (11 sts)
Row 10: K1, M1R, K9, M1L, K1. (13 sts)
Row 12: SSK, K9, K2tog. (11 sts)
Row 14: SSK, K7, K2tog. (9 sts)
Row 16: (SSK) 2 times, K1, (K2tog) 2 times. (5 sts)
Row 18: SSK, K1, pull 1st st over, K2tog, pull 1st st over, cut yarn, leaving a tail 8-10 inches for seaming to body, and pull through last st.

Three small lines are embroidered across back of carapace with color A. This can be done now or after seaming it to the body. Position on top of body and seam in place with cast-off tail. Carapace should extend ⅛-¼"/0.3-0.6 cm beyond body on sides, and the cast-off edge should sit just below P row at neck.

Four to six green-blue or cream colored eggs with brown and grey speckles are laid up in a cup nest made of twigs, grass, and lined with hair ♥

Eggs are incubated by the female for 13 days.

NEST & EGGS OF BLACK-HEADED BUNTING

*Sighted at Central Balkan National Park, Bulgaria

Nest is built in a low bush or shrub and is sometimes decorated with bright flowers.

Nestlings fledge after 10 days!

Nest and Eggs of Black-Headed Buntings

✳ Nest

SIZE

4.5"/11.5 cm wide
2"/5 cm tall

YARN

Cascade Aereo, #4 medium weight, 47% merino wool/31% baby alpaca/22% nylon, 240 yd./220 m per 3.5 oz./100 g skein
  or
Cascade 220, #4 medium weight, 100% Peruvian Highland wool, 220 yd./200 m per 3.5 oz./100 g skein

  • Any 3 colors held together; 60 yd./55 m total

NEEDLES

US size 10½/6.5 m dpns

NOTIONS

Darning needle

✳ Eggs

SIZE

1.25"/3 cm long
¾"/2 cm wide

YARN

Cascade Nifty Cotton, #4 medium weight, 100% cotton, 185 yd./169.5 m per 3.5 oz./100 g skein

  • A suggestions: 09 Buff; 13 Soft Blue (egg); 5 yd./4.5 m
  • B: 20 Chocolate (spots); 1 yd/1 m

NEEDLES

US size 3/3.25 dpns

NOTIONS

Darning needle
Stuffing

INSTRUCTIONS

• Nest

Using 3 strands of yarn held together, CO 6 sts onto 3 larger-size dpns and join in the round.

Rnd 1: P all sts.
Rnd 2: (Kfb) 6 times. (12 sts)
Rnd 3: P all sts.
Rnd 4: (Kfb, K1) 6 times. (18 sts)
Rnd 5: P all sts.
Rnd 6: (Kfb, K2) 6 times. (24 sts)
Rnd 7: P all sts.
Rnd 8: (Kfb, K3) 6 times. (30 sts)
Rnd 9: P all sts.
Rnd 10: (Kfb, K4) 6 times. (36 sts)
Rnds 11–27: K all sts.
Rnd 28: (K2tog, K4) 6 times. (30 sts)
Rnd 29: P all sts.
Rnd 30: (K2tog, K3) 6 times. (24 sts)
Rnd 31: P all sts.
Rnd 32: (K2tog, K2) 6 times. (18 sts)
Rnd 33: P all sts.
Rnd 34: (K2tog, K1) 6 times. (12 sts)
Rnd 35: P all sts.
Rnd 36: (K2tog) 6 times. (6 sts)

Cut yarn, thread through remaining live sts, and pull closed. Weave in both loose ends. Push one side of the ball down inside the other, using your fingers to shape into a nest.

• Eggs

Work begins at smaller end of egg. With color A, CO 6 sts onto 3 smaller-size dpns and join in the round.

Rnd 1: K all sts.
Rnd 2: (M1, K2) 3 times. (9 sts)
Rnd 3: K all sts.
Rnd 4: (M1, K3) 3 times. (12 sts)
Rnds 5–8: K all sts.
Rnd 9: (K2tog, K2) 3 times. (9 sts)
Rnd 10: K all sts.

Stuff egg fully before working the final round.

Rnd 11: (K2tog, K1) 3 times. (6 sts)

Cut yarn, thread through remaining live sts, and pull closed. Weave in loose ends. Embroider spots with color B.

Raccoons have remarkably sensitive hands, with five long fingers and long nails. They don't have thumbs so can't grasp objects with one hand - but they use both forepaws together to lift and manipulate objects.

* Sighted near Upper Gauley River, West Virginia

COMMON RACCOON

The mask of black fur that covers its eyes is its most familiar feature. It is believed that the dark fur may help reduce glare and enhance night vision

Because its hind legs are longer than its front legs, a raccoon often appears hunched when they walk or run.

these are the tracks he makes

The Common raccoon is nocturnal, mostly foraging and feeding at night.

Common Raccoon

SIZE

18"/45.5 cm long (including tail)
7"/18 cm tall

YARN

Cascade Aereo, #4 medium weight, 47% merino wool/31% baby alpaca/22% nylon, 240 yd./220 m per 3.5 oz./100 g skein
- A suggestions: 02 Charcoal; 03 Silver; 05 Doeskin Heather (body, legs, head); 150 yd./137 m
- B: 05 Doeskin Heather (paws; tail stripes); 20 yd./18 m
- C: 01 Jet (tail stripes, face stripe); 10 yd./9 m
- D: 04 Ecru (face); 5 yd./4.5 m

NEEDLES

US size 5/3.75 mm dpns

NOTIONS

Darning needle
Stitch marker (optional)
Stuffing
Wire pet brush (optional)

INSTRUCTIONS

• Front Right Leg

Work begins at bottom of leg and proceeds upward. CO 13 sts with color A onto 3 dpns. Join in the round by slipping the first CO st onto the 3rd needle and then pulling the 2nd stitch (formerly the last st) over it and off the needle; 12 sts remain.

Rnds 1–4: K all sts.
Rnd 5: (K1, M1R, K4, M1L, K1) 2 times. (16 sts)
Rnds 6–9: K all sts.
Rnd 10: (K1, M1R, K6, M1L, K1) 2 times. (20 sts)
Rnds 11–14: K all sts.
Rnd 15: (K1, M1R, K8, M1L, K1) 2 times. (24 sts)
Rnds 16–19: K all sts.
Rnd 20: K1, M1R, K8, SSK, K2, K2tog, K8, M1L, K1.
Rnd 21: K all sts.
Rnd 22: K1, M1R, K22, M1L, K1. (26 sts)
Rnds 23–24: K all sts.
Rnd 25: K1, M1R, K9, SSK, K2, K2tog, K9, M1L, K1.
Rnd 26: K all sts.
Rnd 27: K1, M1R, K24, M1L, K1. (28 sts)
Rnds 28–29: K all sts.
Rnd 30: K1, M1R, K10, SSK, K2, K2tog, K10, M1L, K1.
Rnd 31: K all sts.
Rnd 32: K1, M1R, K26, M1L, K1. (30 sts)
Rnds 33–34: K all sts.

Cast off first 3 sts, K11, cast off next 14 sts, cut yarn and pull through last st. 12 live sts remain on needle. Rejoin color A at first st on P side of work. The following rows are worked flat; turn work after each one.

Row 1: P all sts.
Row 2: Slip 1, K11.
Row 3: Slip 1, P11.

Repeat rows 2 and 3 four more times for a total of 11 rows worked in stockinette stitch. Cut yarn. Place live sts on scrap yarn or a spare dpn and set aside.

• Front Left Leg

Work all rounds 1–34 the same as the right leg. Cast off first 15 sts, K11, cast off next 2 sts, cut yarn and pull through last st. 12 sts remain on needle. Repeat all instructions for the flat part of the leg.

Place 12 sts from each leg onto a dpn. With RS facing, join together with a 3-needle bind-off.

• Body

Sts are picked up along the top edge in the back and down the inside of each leg to begin shaping the body. Using 5 dpns (4 to pick up sts and 1 working dpn) helps pick up and organize the sts for the first several rounds.

Hold legs together so that the "elbow" bend is pointing toward the back. Begin on the elbow side and at the top/center where sts were joined with the 3-needle bind-off. With RS facing, PU 10 sts along the back edge from the center to the top of the right leg opening. With a 2nd dpn, 18 sts are now picked up down the inside of the right leg: 9 at a downward angle toward the center and then 9 straight down the center of the leg, ending up at or slightly below the "elbow." These picked-up sts do not have to be exact, as long as 18 are

picked up from the top of the leg opening down to the elbow.

With a 3rd dpn, do the same thing in reverse. PU 18 sts on the inside of the left leg: 9 straight up the middle and then 9 at an angle from the middle to the top of the leg opening. With a 4th dpn, PU 10 sts along the back edge of the leg piece from the leg opening to the center seam. 56 sts (EOR).

Picking up sts along the inside of the legs will cause them to look misshapen at first. Once the body is completed and stuffed, the elbow will point backward and the increases and decreases will run in straight lines down the center of the front and back of both front legs. Join sts in the round.

Rnds 1–5: K all sts.
Rnd 6: K2, M1R, K4, M1R, K44, M1L, K4, M1L, K2. (60 sts)
Rnd 7: K all sts.
Rnd 8: K2, M1R, K4, M1R, K48, M1L, K4, M1L, K2. (64 sts)
Rnd 9: K all sts.

The majority of the body is worked with short rows. These will shape the hump in your raccoon's back and change the direction of the sts so that they flow straight down into the back legs.

Row 1: K4, w&t.
Row 2: P8, w&t.
Row 3: K10, w&t.
Row 4: P12, w&t.
Row 5: K14, w&t.
Row 6: P16, w&t.
Row 7: K18, w&t.
Row 8: P20, w&t.
Row 9: K22, w&t.
Row 10: P24, w&t.
Row 11: K26, w&t.
Row 12: P28, w&t.
Row 13: K30, w&t.
Row 14: P32, w&t.
Row 15: K34, w&t.
Row 16: P36, w&t.
Row 17: K38, w&t.
Row 18: P40, w&t.
Row 19: K42, w&t.
Row 20: P44, w&t.
Row 21: K46, w&t.
Row 22: P48, w&t.

Row 23: K46, w&t.
Row 24: P44, w&t.
Row 25: K42, w&t.
Row 26: P40, w&t.
Row 27: K38, w&t.
Row 28: P36, w&t.
Row 29: K34, w&t.
Row 30: P32, w&t.
Row 31: K30, w&t.
Row 32: P28, w&t.
Row 33: K26, w&t.
Row 34: P24, w&t.
Row 35: K22, w&t.
Row 36: P20, w&t.
Row 37: K18, w&t.
Row 38: P16, w&t.
Row 39: K14, w&t.
Row 40: P12, w&t.
Row 41: K10, w&t.
Row 42: P8, w&t.
Row 43: K4 (EOR).

Knitting in the round is resumed for the next 9 rounds.

Rnd 44: K all sts.

Rnd 45: K62, place last 2 sts on scrap yarn, CO 2 new sts to EOR.

Rnd 46: Add first 2 sts in round to same piece of scrap yarn, CO 2 new sts to working needle (first 2 sts in rnd), K62. (64 sts)

Rnds 47–52: K all sts.

Rows 53–61 are more short rows to shape the back of the body:

Row 53: K4, w&t.

Row 54: P8, w&t.

Row 55: K10, w&t.

Row 56: P12, w&t.

Row 57: K14, w&t.

Row 58: P16, w&t.

Row 59: K18, w&t.

Row 60: P20, w&t.

Row 61: K10 (EOR).

Rnd 62: K all sts.

• Back Right Leg

Setup: K32, place remaining 32 on scrap yarn. Join first 32 sts in the round. K8, place a st marker or arrange sts on the needles with a break here to designate new EOR.

Rnd 1: K all sts.

Rnd 2: (K1, K2tog, K10, SSK, K1) 2 times. (28 sts)

Rnd 3: K all sts.

Rnd 4: (K1, K2tog, K8, SSK, K1) 2 times. (24 sts)

Rnd 5: K all sts.

Rnd 6: (K1, K2tog, K6, SSK, K1) 2 times. (20 sts)

Rnd 7: K all sts.

Rnd 8: (K1, K2tog, K4, SSK, K1) 2 times. (16 sts)

Rnd 9: K all sts.

Rnd 10: (K1, K2tog, K2, SSK, K1) 2 times. (12 sts)

Rnds 11–15: K all sts.

Cut color A.

• Back Paws (make 2 the same)

Join color B.

Rnd 1: K all sts.

Rows 2–6 are short rows to shape the heel.

Row 2: K1, w&t.

Row 3: P2, w&t.

Row 4: K3, w&t.

Row 5: P4, w&t.

Row 6: K2 (EOR).

Knitting in the round is now resumed.

Rnds 7–13: K all sts.

Rnd 14: K3, SSK, K2, K2tog, K3. (10 sts)

Cut yarn, thread through live sts, and pull closed. Weave in loose end.

• Back Left Leg

Setup: Place live sts from scrap yarn onto 3 dpns. With RS facing, rejoin color A at first st (bottom of raccoon); K32. Join sts in the round. K24 sts; place a st marker here, or arrange sts on the needles with a break here to designate new EOR. Work all rows of leg and paw the same as for the right leg.

• Tail

Two colors are carried inside the tail while working; do not cut yarn after each stripe.

Setup: Place 4 sts from scrap yarn onto 1 dpn. With RS facing, join color C at first st; K4. With a 2nd dpn, PU 6 sts around the edge of the opening from the last st you just knitted to bottom/center (EOR). With a 3rd dpn, PU 6 more sts from bottom/center to first original st at the top; K10; 16 sts.

With color C:

Rnds 1–2: K all sts.

With color B:

Rnds 3–6: K all sts.

With color C:

Rnd 7: (M1, K4) 4 times. (20 sts)

Rnds 8–9: K all sts.

Continue to knit all sts and alternate colors: (color C for 3 rounds and color B for 4 rounds) until the last round of the 5th color B stripe; then begin alternating decrease rounds with plain knit rounds.

Decrease round: K1, K2tog, K to last 3 sts, SSK, K1.

Next round: K all sts.

Repeat last two rounds 4 more times while continuing the color pattern; then K all sts for 1 round. Cut yarn, thread through remaining live sts, and pull closed. Weave in loose ends.

• Front Paws

Sts are picked up around the bottom edge of front legs to work the paws. It's important to start picking up sts at the right place so that the paws will face forward. Begin picking up sts at the center/back of the leg opening. To more easily see where that is, flatten one leg so that the increases/decreases run straight down the front and back. PU a total of 8 sts around the opening: 2 for every 3 of the original CO sts. Join in the round.

Rnds 1–3: K all sts.

Rows 4–8 are short rows to shape the heel.

Row 4: K1, w&t.

Row 5: P2, w&t.

Row 6: K3, w&t.

Row 7: P4, w&t.

Row 8: K2 (EOR).

Knitting in the round is resumed.

Rnd 9: K3, (M1, K1) 2 times, K3. (10 sts)

Rnds 10–14: K all sts.

Cut yarn, thread through live sts, and pull closed. Weave in loose end.

• Top of Head

The head is worked in two pieces: top and bottom. The top piece starts off flat; then sts are joined in the round to work the snout. The bottom piece is worked flat and is seamed to the top. Sts are picked up around the edge of the front legs to begin.

Setup: With WS of right leg facing and color A, PUP 5 sts on the top edge of the right leg as follows: 2 sts on the right side of the increases, 1 st in the center of the increases, and 2 sts on the left side of the increases; turn work.

Row 1: Slip 1, K4, turn work.

Row 2: Slip 1, P4, turn work.

Row 3: Slip 1, K4.

PU and knit 1 st along the edge of the work you just completed. PU and knit 9 sts along the edge from the st you just picked up to the center/back.

With a 2nd dpn, PU and knit 1 st exactly in the center/back of neck. This will be in the center of the 3-needle bind-off. Then PU and knit 11 sts to the left of the center down to the increases on the front of the leg. PU and knit 1 st in the center of the increases and 2 sts on the inside of the increases; turn work.

Row 1: Slip 1, P4, turn work.

Row 2: Slip 1, K4, turn work.

Row 3: Slip 1, P4.

PUP 1 st along the edge of the work you just completed, P25 (EOR). 31 sts total: 1 st in the top/center, and 15 on each side. Turn work.

Row 1: SSK, K27, K2tog. (29 sts)

Row 2: Slip 1, P28.

Row 3: Slip 1, K28.

Row 4: Slip 1, P28.

Row 5: SSK, K25, K2tog. (27 sts)

Row 6: Slip 1, P26.

Rows 7–11 are short rows to shape the top of the head:

Row 7: Slip 1, K19, w&t.

Row 8: P13, w&t.

Row 9: K11, w&t.

Row 10: P9, w&t.

Row 11: K18 (EOR).

Cut color A; join color D. A tiny bit of intarsia is used for one stitch only in each row of the following section. It creates the color A stripe that runs vertically down the face from the center stitch. Cut a strand of color A about 15 inches long and use that when you get to the center stitch, as indicated. With the intarsia method of colorwork, always bring the new color over the old one when changing colors to prevent a gap from forming between them.

Row 12: P13; P1 color A; P13.

Row 13: SSK, K11; K1 color A; K11, K2tog. (25 sts)

Row 14: Slip 1, P11; P1 color A; P12.

Cut color D; join color C.

Row 15: K5, SSK, K2, SSK, K1; K1 color A; K1, K2tog, K2, K2tog, K5. (21 sts)

Row 16: Slip 1, P9; P1 color A; P10.

Row 17: SSK, K8; K1 color A; K8, K2tog. (19 sts)

Row 18: Slip 1, P8; P1 color A; P9.

Row 19: Slip 1, K2, (SSK, K1) 2 times; K1 color A; (K1, K2tog) 2 times, K3. (15 sts)

The remainder of the head is knit in the round. Arrange sts on 3 dpns and join in the round by slipping the first st onto the 3rd needle and then pulling the 2nd stitch (formerly the last st) over it and off the needle; 14 sts remain. Continue working with color C (with one st of color A) for the first round.

Rnd 20: K6, K1 color A, K7.

Cut both colors A and C now and join color D; the remainder of the head is worked in the round with color D.

Rnd 21: K all sts.

Rnd 22: K2tog, K10, SSK. (12 sts)

Rnds 23–24: K all sts.

Rnd 25: K2tog, K8, SSK. (10 sts)

Rnds 26–27: K all sts.

Rnd 28: K2tog, K6, SSK. (8 sts)

Rnd 29: K2tog, K4, SSK. (6 sts)

Cut yarn, thread through remaining live sts, and pull closed. Weave in loose ends.

• Stuff Body and Seam Front Legs Closed

The raccoon can now be stuffed. The body and legs should be stuffed fully; the tail should be stuffed more loosely, and the paws should have very little stuffing in them and be more flat than round. Use a dpn to help move the stuffing down into the legs and tail and to shift the stuffing around in the center body cavity.

The front legs are now seamed together with color A. Begin at the bottom of the opening, seam legs together leaving about ½"/1.25 cm from the increases on each leg. Continue upward toward the head until ½"/1.25 cm from the top of the legs.

• Bottom of Head

The bottom of the head is worked separately and seamed to the top piece. CO 4 sts of color A onto 1 dpn. All rows are worked flat.
Row 1: Slip 1, P3.
Row 2: Slip 1, K3.
Row 3: Slip 1, P3.
Row 4: Slip 1, K3.
Row 5: Slip 1, P3.
Row 6: Slip 1, M1L, K2, M1R, K1. (6 sts)
Row 7: Slip 1, P5.
Row 8: Slip 1, M1L, K4, M1R, K1. (8 sts)

Row 9: Slip 1, P7.
Row 10: Slip 1, M1L, K6, M1R, K1. (10 sts)
Row 11: Slip 1, P9.
Row 12: Slip 1, K9.
Row 13: Slip 1, P9.
Row 14: Slip 1, K9.
Row 15: Slip 1, P9.
Row 16: Slip 1, K9.
Row 17: Slip 1, P10.
Row 18: Slip 1, SSK, K4, K2tog, K1. (8 sts)
Row 19: Slip 1, P7.
Row 20: Slip 1, SSK, K2, K2tog, K1. (6 sts)
Row 21: Slip 1, P5.
Row 22: Slip 1, K5.
Row 23: Slip 1, P5.
Row 24: Slip 1, SSK, K2tog, K1. (4 sts)
Row 25: Slip 1, P3.

Cast off, cut yarn, and pull through last st. Place CO edge at end of leg seam and seam in place, stuffing head fully just before seaming all the way closed. The top of the head and "cheeks" should be full and rounded; the bottom of the head should be flat and without a bulge.

• Ears (make 2 the same)

With color A, CO 11 sts onto 3 dpns. Join in the round by slipping the first CO st onto the 3rd needle and then pulling the 2nd stitch (formerly the last st) over it and off the needle; 10 sts remain.
Rnds 1–2: K all sts.
Rnd 3: K2tog, K6, SSK. (8 sts)
Rnds 4–5: K all sts.

Cut yarn, thread through remaining live sts, and pull closed. Weave in loose end. Seam CO edge to head.

• Finishing

Embroider nose with color C. The eyes are also embroidered with color C; even though they are placed on the color C stripe and therefore don't stand out very much, the shape is still slightly visible. A small dot of color D can be added.

The "cheeks" can be felted slightly with a wire brush.

Holding back legs together, seam hole between them closed from top to bottom.

TRACKS

In the fall, as temperatures cool and food becomes scarcer, grizzlies dig dens in the sides of hills.

They have long rounded claws (the size of human fingers).

They are good swimmers and fast runners, reaching speeds as high as 35 mph over land.

GRIZZLY BEAR

*Sighted at Long Mountain Lake Selkirk Mountains, Idaho

When standing upright on their hind legs, they can reach 8ft tall

Grizzlies have an astute sense of smell. Even better than a hound dog

Grizzly Bear

SIZE

13"/33 cm tall
6"/15 cm wide

YARN

Cascade Aereo, #4 medium weight, 47% merino wool/31% baby alpaca/22% nylon, 240 yd./220 m per 3.5 oz./100 g skein
- A suggestions: 07 Mocha Heather; 08 Camel (body); 150 yd./137 m
- B suggestions: 05 Doeskin Heather; 08 Camel (muzzle); 2 yd./2 m

NEEDLES

US size 5/3.75 mm dpns

NOTIONS

Darning needle
Scrap of black or brown yarn (to embroider eyes and nose)
Stuffing

INSTRUCTIONS

• Body

Work begins at center/back of neckline. With color A, CO 31 sts onto 3 dpns. Join in the round by slipping the first CO st onto the 3rd needle and then pulling the 2nd stitch (formerly the last st) over it and off the needle; 30 sts remain.

Rnd 1 and all odd rounds through 39: K all sts.
Rnd 2: K5, M1R, K8, M1L, K4, M1R, K8, M1L, K5. (34 sts)
Rnd 4: K6, M1R, K8, M1L, K6, M1R, K8, M1L, K6. (38 sts)
Rnd 6: K7, M1R, K8, M1L, K8, M1R, K8, M1L, K7. (42 sts)
Rnd 8: K8, M1R, K8, M1L, K10, M1R, K8, M1L, K8. (46 sts)
Rnd 10: K9, M1R, K8, M1L, K12, M1R, K8, M1L, K9. (50 sts)
Rnd 12: K10, M1R, K8, M1L, K14, M1R, K8, M1L, K10. (54 sts)
Rnd 14: K11, M1R, K8, M1L, K16, M1R, K8, M1L, K11. (58 sts)
Rnd 16: K12, M1R, K8, M1L, K18, M1R, K8, M1L, K12. (62 sts)
Rnd 18: K13, M1R, K8, M1L, K20, M1R, K8, M1L, K13. (66 sts)
Rnd 20: K13, place 10 sts on scrap yarn, K20, place 10 sts on scrap yarn, K13. (46 sts)
Rnds 21-40: K all sts.
Rnd 41: K12, (M1, K2) 4 times, K6, (K2, M1) 4 times, K12. (54 sts)
Rnds 42-43: K all sts.
Rnd 44: K14, (M1, K2) 3 times, K14, (K2, M1) 3 times, K14. (60 sts)
Rnds 45-56: K all sts.

• Right Leg

Setup: K30, place 30 on scrap yarn. Arrange first 30 onto 3 dpns; join in the round.
Rnd 1 and all odd rounds through 15: K all sts.
Rnd 2: K2tog, K2, K2tog, K18, SSK, K2, SSK. (26 sts)
Rnd 4: K2tog, K2, K2tog, K14, SSK, K2, SSK. (22 sts)
Rnd 6: K2tog, K2, K2tog, K10, SSK, K2, SSK. (18 sts)
Rnd 8: K2tog, K2, K2tog, K6, SSK, K2, SSK. (14 sts)
Rnd 10: K2tog, K10, SSK. (12 sts)
Rnds 11-16: K all sts.

• Right Paw

Rows 1-9 are short rows to shape the heel. Do not wrap sts before turning. Working in the round is resumed in round 10.
Setup: K2 (new EOR). Place a st marker or arrange sts with a break here to designate the EOR.
Row 1: K1, turn work.
Row 2: Slip 1, P1, turn work.
Row 3: Slip 1, K2, turn work.
Row 4: Slip 1, P3, turn work.
Row 5: Slip 1, K4, turn work.
Row 6: Slip 1, P5, turn work.
Row 7: Slip 1, K6, turn work.
Row 8: Slip 1, P7, turn work.
Row 9: Slip 1, K3.
Rnd 10: K4, M1L in the gap, K4, M1R in the gap, K4. (14 sts)
Rnds 11-14: K all sts.
Rnd 15: (K2tog) 7 times. (7 sts)
Cut yarn, thread through remaining live sts, and pull closed. Weave in loose end.

• Left Leg

Setup: Place 30 sts from scrap yarn onto 3 dpns. With RS facing, rejoin working yarn at 1st st; K30. Join sts in the round and repeat all rnds 1–16, as for the right leg.

• Left Paw

Setup: K19; new EOR. Place st marker or arrange sts so that there is a break in the sts at this point. Repeat all instructions the same as for the right paw.

• Arms (make 2 the same)

Setup: Place 10 sts from scrap yarn onto 2 dpns. With RS facing, rejoin working yarn at 5th st; K5. PU 8 new sts around opening, K5. 18 sts (EOR).

Rnds 1–10: K all sts.
Rnd 11: K7, SSK, K2tog, K7. (16 sts)
Rnds 12–13: K all sts.
Rnd 14: K6, SSK, K2tog, K6. (14 sts)
Rnds 15–19: K all sts.
Rnd 20: K5, SSK, K2tog, K5. (12 sts)
Rnds 21–23: K all sts.
Rnd 24: (M1, K6) 2 times. (14 sts)
Rnds 25–27: K all sts.
Rnd 26: (K2tog, K5) 2 times. (12 sts)

Cut yarn, thread through live sts, and pull closed. Stuff legs, body, and arms moderately, using a dpn from the outside to distribute the stuffing evenly. Paws should be stuffed very little and flattened.

• Head

Sts are now picked up in the original CO sts to work the head. Begin at the 1st CO st (center/back of neck). The increases can be made by inserting needle into the purl bump on the inside of work after every 3 sts.

Rnd 1: (PU 3, M1) 10 times. (40 sts)

Rnds 2–16: K all sts.

Rnd 17: K10, K2tog, K16, K2tog, K10. (38 sts)

Rnds 18–19: K all sts.

Rnd 20: K10, K2tog, K14, K2tog, K10. (36 sts)

Rnds 21–22: K all sts.

Rnd 23: (K2tog) 18 times. (18 sts)

Rnd 24: K all sts.

   Add any stuffing still needed to the body, arms, or legs now. Stuff head.

Rnd 25: (K2tog) 9 times. (9 sts)

   Cut yarn, thread through remaining live sts, and pull closed. Weave in loose end.

• Muzzle

The muzzle is worked separately and seamed to front of head. With color B, CO 11 sts onto 3 dpns. Join in the round by slipping the first CO st onto the 3rd needle and then pulling the 2nd stitch (formerly the last st) over it and off the needle; 10 sts remain.

Rnd 1: K all sts.

Rnd 2: K1, M1R, K8, M1L, K1. (12 sts)

Rnds 3–4: K all sts.

Rnd 5: K1, M1R, K10, M1L, K1. (14 sts)

Rnds 6–8: K all sts.

   Cut color B; join color A and continue below.

Rnd 9: K1, (M1, K2) 6 times, M1, K1. (21 sts)

Rnds 10–12: K all sts.

Rnd 13: K1, (M1, K3) 6 times, M1, K2. (28 sts)

Rnds 14–16: K all sts.

   Cast off all sts loosely. Turn piece inside out and use CO tail to seam end of snout closed, maintaining the angled slope; turn right-side out again. Add stuffing to the entire piece. Seam to front of head with color A, stretching out the cast-off edge in all directions to minimize its appearance while keeping it centered. It may help to run a basting seam around the edge first. The first CO st should be centered at the front of the neck.

• Ears

Ears are worked separately and seamed to head. CO 11 sts with color A onto 3 dpns. Join in the round by slipping the first CO st onto the 3rd needle and then pulling the 2nd stitch (formerly the last st) over it and off the needle; 10 sts remain.

Rnds 1–3: K all sts.
Rnd 4: (K2tog, K3) 2 times. (8 sts)

Cut yarn, thread through remaining live sts, and pull closed. Flatten ear front to back and pinch at bottom to create a slight hollow in the front/center. Seam the CO edge to head with CO tail.

• Tail

Tail is worked separately and seamed to body. CO 11 sts with color A onto 3 dpns. Join in the round by slipping the first CO st onto the 3rd needle and then pulling the 2nd stitch (formerly the last st) over it and off the needle; 10 sts remain.

Rnds 1–8: K all sts.
Rnd 9: (K2tog, K3) 2 times. (8 sts)

Cut yarn, thread through remaining live sts, and pull closed. Stuff loosely and seam CO edge and top half of sides to back of bear; the bottom tip should be at the level of the crotch between legs.

• Finishing

To accentuate the separation between body and legs, use a darning needle to add a running stitch with color A. This straight line will run diagonally in the top fabric from center point between legs to about 5 rows below armpits. Pull to cinch slightly; repeat on the other side.

Hold legs together and seam hole between them closed in a vertical line.

Embroider nose and eyes with scrap of black or brown yarn.

Arms can be bent and tacked into place on the front of body with color A (optional).

CHIMPANZEE

* Sighted at Tacugama Chimpanzee Sanctuary, Sierra Leone West Africa

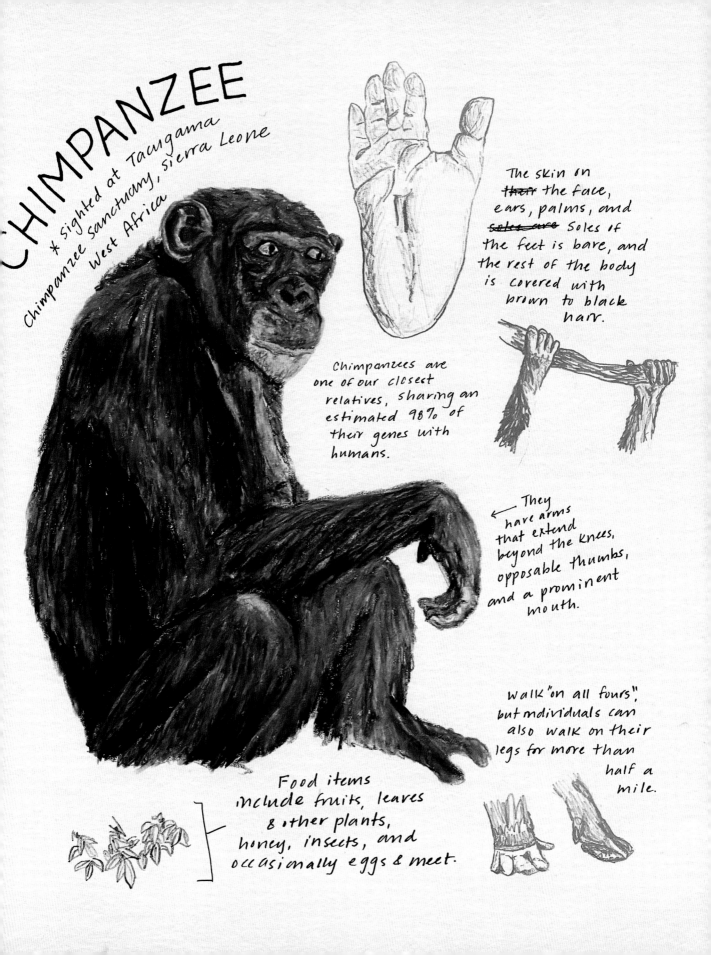

The skin on ~~their~~ the face, ears, palms, and ~~soles are~~ soles of the feet is bare, and the rest of the body is covered with brown to black hair.

Chimpanzees are one of our closest relatives, sharing an estimated 98% of their genes with humans.

← They have arms that extend beyond the knees, opposable thumbs, and a prominent mouth.

Walk "on all fours" but individuals can also walk on their legs for more than half a mile.

Food items include fruits, leaves & other plants, honey, insects, and occasionally eggs & meat.

Chimpanzee

SIZE

13"/33 cm tall
6"/15 cm wide

YARN

Cascade Aereo, #4 medium weight, 47% merino wool/31% baby alpaca/22% nylon, 240 yd./220 m per 3.5 oz./100 g skein

- A suggestions: 01 Jet; 07 Mocha Heather (body, arms, legs, back of head); 100 yd./91 m

Cascade 220, #4 medium weight, 100% Peruvian Highland wool, 220 yd./200 m per 3.5 oz./100 g skein

Color B will always be held double in this pattern.

- B suggestions: 1033 Nectarine; 8021 Beige (hands, feet, face); 30 yd./27.5 m

NEEDLES

US size 5/3.75 mm dpns

NOTIONS

7.5 mm brown safety eyes
Darning needle
Scrap of black yarn for embroidering nostrils
Scrap of reddish yarn for embroidering mouth
Stuffing

INSTRUCTIONS

• Body

Work begins at center/back of neck. With color A, CO 21 sts onto 3 dpns. Join in the round by slipping the first CO st onto the 3rd needle and then pulling the 2nd stitch (formerly the last st) over it and off the needle; 20 sts remain.
Rnd 1: K all sts.
Rnd 2: K7, (M1L, K2) 2 times, (M1R, K2) 2 times, K5. (24 sts)
Rnds 3–5: K all sts.
Rnd 6: K9, (M1L, K2) 2 times, (M1R, K2) 2 times, K7. (28 sts)
Rnds 7–9: K all sts.
Rnd 10: K11, (M1L, K2) 2 times, (M1R, K2) 2 times, K9. (32 sts)
Rnds 11–13: K all sts.

Rnd 14: K13, (M1L, K2) 2 times, (M1R, K2) 2 times, K11. (36 sts)
Rnds 15–17: K all sts.
Rnd 18: K15, (M1L, K2) 2 times, (M1R, K2), 2 times, K13. (40 sts)
Rnds 19–21: K all sts.
Rnd 22: K17, (M1L, K2) 2 times, (M1R, K2) 2 times, K15. (44 sts)
Rnds 23–34: K all sts.
Rnd 35: K15, (SSK, K2) 2 times, (K2tog, K2) 2 times, K13. (40 sts)
Rnds 36–43: K all sts.

• Right Buttock

Continuing from body sts.
Row 1: K5, w&t.
Row 2: P2, w&t.
Row 3: K4, w&t.
Row 4: P6, w&t.
Row 5: K4, w&t.
Row 6: P2, w&t.
Row 7: K4, w&t.
Row 8: P6, w&t.
Row 9: K19, place last 20 sts on a piece of scrap yarn.

• Right Leg

Arrange the first 20 sts on 3 dpns and join in the round.
Rnds 1–5: K all sts.
Rnd 6: K2tog, K16, SSK. (18 sts)
Rnds 7–9: K all sts.
Rnd 10: K2tog, K14, SSK. (16 sts)
Rnds 11–13: K all sts.
Rnd 14: K2tog, K12, SSK. (14 sts)
Rnds 15–16: K all sts.
Rnd 17: K2tog, K10, SSK. (12 sts)
The short rows below will shape the knee.
Row 18: K9, w&t.
Row 19: P2, w&t.
Row 20: K3, w&t.
Row 21: P4, w&t.
Row 22: K3, w&t.
Row 23: P2, w&t.
Row 24: K3, w&t.
Row 25: P4, w&t.
Rnd 26: K6 (EOR).
Rnds 27–38: K all sts.

• Right Foot

Cut color A, join color B held double. Rows 2–9 are short rows to shape the heel.

Rnd 1: K all sts.
Row 2: K3, w&t.
Row 3: P2, w&t.
Row 4: K3, w&t.
Row 5: P4, w&t.
Row 6: K3, w&t.
Row 7: P2, w&t.
Row 8: K3, w&t.
Row 9: P4, w&t (EOR).
Rnd 10: K all sts.
Rnd 11: K4, K2tog, K4, SSK. (10 sts)
Rnds 12–13: K all sts.
Rnd 14: K9, place last st in round together with the first st in next round on a piece of scrap yarn. (8 sts)
Rnds 15–16: K all sts.

Cut yarn, thread through remaining live sts, and pull closed. Place 2 sts from scrap yarn onto 1 dpn. Rejoin color B at first st, K2. Work 2 rows of a 2-st I-cord. Cut yarn, thread through 2 live sts, and pull closed; weave in loose ends. The hands and feet are not stuffed.

• Left Buttock

Arrange 20 sts from scrap yarn onto 3 dpns. With WS facing, rejoin color A at st closest to the right buttock (formerly the last st in round), leaving a tail long enough to close the hole between the legs at a later point.

Row 1: P5, w&t.
Row 2: K2, w&t.
Row 3: P4, w&t.
Row 4: K6, w&t.
Row 5: P4, w&t.
Row 6: K2, w&t.
Row 7: P4, w&t.
Row 8: K6, slip last st.
Join sts in the round.

• Left Leg

Rnds 1–6: K all sts.
Rnd 7: K2tog, K16, SSK. (18 sts)
Rnds 8–10: K all sts.
Rnd 11: K2tog, K14, SSK. (16 sts)
Rnds 12–14: K all sts.
Rnd 15: K2tog, K12, SSK. (14 sts)
Rnds 16–17: K all sts.
Rnd 18: K2tog, K10, SSK. (12 sts)

The short rows in rows 19–26 will shape the knee.
Row 19: K3, w&t.
Row 20: P2, w&t.
Row 21: K3, w&t.
Row 22: P4, w&t.
Row 23: K3, w&t.
Row 24: P2, w&t.
Row 25: K3, w&t.
Row 26: P4, w&t.
Rnds 27–38: K all sts.

• Left Foot

Cut color A; join color B held double. Rows 2–9 are short rows to shape the heel.

Rnd 1: K all sts.
Row 2: K10, w&t.
Row 3: P2, w&t.
Row 4: K3, w&t.
Row 5: P4, w&t.
Row 6: K3, w&t.
Row 7: P2, w&t.

Row 8: K3, w&t.
Row 9: P5, w&t, K6 (EOR).
Rnd 10: K4, K2tog, K4, SSK.
Rnds 11–12: K all sts.
Rnd 13: K9, place last st in round together with the first st in next round on a piece of scrap yarn. (8 sts)
Rnds 14–15: K all sts.

Cut yarn, thread through remaining live sts, and pull closed. Place 2 sts from scrap yarn onto 1 dpn. Rejoin color B at first st, K2. Work 2 rows of a 2-st I-cord. Cut yarn, thread through 2 live sts, and pull closed. Weave in loose ends.

Body and legs are stuffed now.

• Head

Sts are now picked up in the original CO sts to work the head. Beginning at the first CO st (center/back of neck), PU 20 sts with color A and 3 dpns. Join sts in the round.
Rnd 1: (Kfb) 20 times. (40 sts)
Rnds 2–3: K all sts.
Row 4: K6, w&t.
Row 5: P12, w&t.
Row 6: K14, w&t.
Row 7: P16, w&t.
Row 8: K18, w&t.
Row 9: P20, w&t.
Row 10: K22, w&t.
Row 11: P24, w&t.
Row 12: K12 (EOR).
Rnd 13: K all sts.
Rnd 14: K6, (K2tog) 7 times, (SSK) 7 times, K6. (26 sts)

Rows 15–18 are worked flat on the first and last 6 sts of the round only; turn work after each row.
Row 15: K6.
Row 16: Slip 1, P11.
Row 17: (SSK) 3 times, (K2tog) 3 times. (20 sts)
Row 18: Cast off 5, cut color A and pull through last st. (14 sts)

The remainder of the head is worked flat with color B yarn held double. With WS facing, join yarn at first st on far right.
Row 19: P14.
Row 20: K6, M1L, K2, M1R, w&t. (16 sts)
Row 21: P4, w&t.
Row 22: K4, w&t.
Row 23: P4, w&t.
Row 24: K5, w&t.
Row 25: P6, w&t.

Row 26: K6, w&t.
Row 27: P6, w&t.
Row 28: K7, w&t.
Row 29: P8, w&t.
Row 30: K9, w&t.
Row 31: P10, w&t.
Row 32: K1, (SSK) 2 times, (K2tog) 2 times, K2, w&t. (12 sts)
Row 33: P8, w&t.
Row 34: (SSK) 2 times, (K2tog) 2 times, K1, w&t. (8 sts)
Row 35: P6, w&t.
Row 36: K1, SSK, K2tog, K2. (6 sts)
Row 37: P all sts.
Row 38: K all sts.
Row 39: P all sts.
Row 40: K all sts.
Row 41: P all sts.
Row 42: Cast off all sts.

Cut yarn and pull through last st. Weave in loose ends. Stuff head, adding more stuffing to the body if needed at this time.

Top ¼"/0.6 cm of color B work is folded to the back, forming a forehead, and then the top edge of forehead is seamed to the cast-off color A sts. Attach safety eyes through holes on each side, and then seam holes closed with color A.

The nose and eyebrow ridge are embroidered with color B. Two tiny black lines can be made for the nostrils at the bottom of the nose.

The mouth is embroidered with a single ply of red yarn.

• Ears (make 2 the same)

The ears are worked flat and seamed to sides of head. With color B held double, CO 3 sts to 1 dpn.

Row 1: P all sts.
Row 2: K all sts.
Row 3: P all sts.
Row 4: SSK, K1, pass first st over last st and off needle.

Cut yarn and pull through last st. Weave in loose end. Seam CO edge to sides of head with CO tail about 6 rows up from neckline and 4 rows behind eyes.

Add more stuffing (if needed) to the body or legs through the hole between the legs. When stuffing, accentuate the buttocks and knees.

Seam hole between legs closed from side to side with color A.

• Arms (make 2 the same)

The arms are worked separately and then attached to body. With color A, CO 8 sts onto 1 dpn. Rows 1–10 are worked flat, shaping the curve at the top. Sts are then joined in the round for the remainder of the arm and hand.

Row 1: P all sts.
Row 2: K all sts.
Row 3: P all sts.
Row 4: K5, w&t.
Row 5: P2, w&t.
Row 6: K3, w&t.
Row 7: P4, w&t.
Row 8: K5, w&t.
Row 9: P6, w&t.

Row 10: K7 (EOR).

With RS facing and 2 dpns, PU 8 sts around the edge of the work: 2 along the upper edge, 4 along the CO edge, and 2 along the lower edge. 16 sts total (EOR).

Rnds 11–34: K all sts.
Rnd 35: K2tog, K12, SSK. (14 sts)
Rnds 36–39: K all sts.
Rnd 40: K2tog, K10, SSK. (12 sts)
Rnds 41–44: K all sts.
Rnd 45: K2tog, K8, SSK. (10 sts)
Rnds 46–49: K all sts.
Rnd 50: K2tog, K6, SSK. (8 sts)
Rnds 51–56: K all sts.

Cut color A; stuff arm loosely.

• Hands (make 2 the same)

Join color B (held double) at first st.

Rnds 1–5: K all sts.
Rnd 6: K7, place last st in rnd tog with 1st in next rnd on scrap yarn.
Rnds 7–9: K all sts.

Cut yarn, thread through remaining live sts, and pull closed. Place 2 sts from scrap yarn onto 1 dpn. Rejoin color B at first st, K2. Work 1 row of a 2-st I-cord. Cut yarn, thread through 2 live sts, and pull closed. Weave in loose ends.

Arms can be either seamed to body in desired position or attached with a double strand of yarn that runs shoulder to shoulder through the upper chest. The latter method of attaching allows the arms to be flexible.

They bury food in winter caches using a method called scatter hoarding. They are able to locate these caches later using memory and smell.

Eastern gray squirrels once provided food for Native Americans and colonists and are still eaten by some people today.

EASTERN GRAY SQUIRREL

* Sighted at Leister Park Hampstead, Maryland

They build nests made of leaves in the higher branches of large trees.

The tail is used for maintaining balance while it leaps between branches.

Squirrels keep their ever-growing teeth clean and sharp by gnawing on hard branches. This daily ritual can take up to an hour to preform.

Eastern Gray Squirrel

SIZE

6"/15 cm tall
3"/7.5 cm wide

YARN

Cascade 220, #4 medium weight, 100%
Peruvian Highland wool, 220 yd./200 m per
3.5 oz./100 g skein
- A suggestions: 8401 Silver Grey; 8011
  Aspen Heather (back, legs, tail, head, ears);
  120 yd./110 m
- B: 8010 Natural

NEEDLES

US size 4/3.5 mm dpns

NOTIONS

6 mm x 8 mm black oval safety eyes (optional)
Darning needle
Scrap of white yarn for embroidery around eyes
Scrap of pink, beige, or black yarn for
embroidering nose
Stuffing

INSTRUCTIONS

• Body—Back Piece

The body of the squirrel is worked flat in two
separate pieces that are then joined together in
the round to work the base. Work begins at the
neckline for both pieces of the body. With color A,
CO 13 sts onto 1 dpn and work the following rows
back and forth:
Row 1: P all sts.
Row 2: K all sts.
Row 3: P all sts.
Row 4: K6, M1R, K1, M1L, K6. (15 sts)
Row 5: P all sts.
Row 6: K all sts.
Row 7: P all sts.
Row 8: K7, M1R, K1, M1L, K7. (17 sts)
Row 9: P all sts.
Row 10: K all sts.
Row 11: P all sts.
Row 12: K8, M1R, K1, M1L, K8. (19 sts)
Row 13: P all sts.

Row 14: K all sts.
Row 15: P all sts.
Row 16: K15, w&t.
Row 17: P11, w&t.
Row 18: K12, w&t.
Row 19: P13, w&t.
Row 20: K14, w&t.
Row 21: P15, w&t.
Row 22: K13, w&t.
Row 23: P11, w&t.
Row 24: K12, w&t.
Row 25: P13, w&t.
Row 26: K15, w&t.
Row 27: P17, w&t.
Row 28: K18 (EOR).
Row 29: P all sts.
Row 30: K all sts.

Repeat last 2 rows 7 times for a total of 16 rows
worked in stockinette stitch, ending after a RS
row. Set back piece aside while you work the front
piece. Do not cut working yarn.

• Body—Front Piece

With color B, CO 5 sts onto 1 dpn and work the
following rows back and forth.
Row 1: P all sts.
Row 2: K all sts.
Row 3: P all sts.
Row 4: K1, M1R, K3, M1L, K1. (7 sts)
Row 5: P all sts.
Row 6: K all sts.
Row 7: P all sts.
Row 8: K1, M1R, K5, M1L, K1. (9 sts)
Row 9: P all sts.
Row 10: K all sts.
Row 11: P all sts.
Row 12: K1, M1R, K7, M1L, K1. (11 sts)
Row 13: P all sts.
Row 14: K all sts.
Row 15: P all sts.
Row 16: K1, M1R, K9, M1L, K1. (13 sts)
Row 17: P all sts.
Row 18: K all sts.

Repeat last 2 rows 7 times for a total of 16
rows worked in stockinette stitch, ending after a
RS row.

Cut color B, leaving a long tail to seam back and front pieces together after base is worked.

• Base

Arrange live color A sts onto 2 dpns. These sts are now joined in the round with color B sts. Join last color A st (with working yarn) to first color B st; 32 sts total (EOR). The base is worked with color A.

Rnd 1: K all sts.
Rnd 2: (K2, K2tog) 8 times. (24 sts)
Rnd 3: K all sts.
Rnd 4: (K1, K2tog) 8 times. (16 sts)
Rnd 5: K all sts.
Rnd 6: (K2tog) 8 times. (8 sts)

Cut yarn, thread through remaining live sts, and pull closed. Weave in loose end.

• Seaming

The 2 pieces of the body are now seamed together. Beginning at the base and using the color B loose end, seam front and back edges together with a whipstitch for 18 rows from the base upward. You will stop just above the row with the wrap-and-turns. Leave the next 10 rows open for the armhole; then seam closed the last 4 rows above the arm opening. Repeat same on the other side. Weave in loose ends.

Don't stuff the body yet; it's easier to knit the arms if left unstuffed.

• Arms (work same for both)

Beginning at the bottom of the armhole, PU 16 sts around the opening with 3 dpns and color A (EOR). Join sts in the round.

Rnds 1–8: K all sts.
Rnd 9: (SSK) 2 times, K8, (K2tog) 2 times. (12 sts)
Rnd 10: K all sts.
Rnd 11: SSK, K8, K2tog. (10 sts)
Rnd 12: K all sts.
Rnd 13: SSK, K6, K2tog. (8 sts)
Rnd 14: K all sts.
Rnd 15: SSK, K4, K2tog. (6 sts)
Rnd 16: M1R, K5, M1L, K1. (8 sts)
Rnds 17–18: K all sts.

Cut yarn, thread through remaining live sts, and pull closed. Weave in loose end. Use the tail from picking up stitches to seam closed any holes beneath arm.

Stuff body, flattening the base and accentuating the curve in back. Add only a small amount of stuffing to the arms.

• Head

Sts are now picked up in the CO sts of the back piece to work the head. With color A and 2 dpns, begin where colors A and B meet on right side of body, and PU 16 sts in the original color A CO sts: 8 on each side of the center. Note: This is 3 more sts than was originally cast on for the back piece. The first part of the head is worked flat.

Row 1: P all sts.
Row 2: K10, w&t.
Row 3: P4, w&t.
Row 4: K6, w&t.
Row 5: P8, w&t.
Row 6: K10, w&t.
Row 7: P12, w&t.
Row 8: K14 (EOR).
Rnd 9: P all sts.
Rnd 10: (SSK) 2 times, K8, (K2tog) 2 times. (12 sts)

Arrange all sts on 1 dpn. More sts are now picked up along the sides of your work and across color B section of body. They are then joined in the round with remaining live sts at back of head.

Setup: With a 2nd dpn and RS facing, PU 5 sts down the left side of your work and 3 sts in the CO sts at left side of the color B piece. With a 3rd dpn, PU 3 sts on the right side of the color B piece, and 5 sts up the right side of your work; 28 sts (EOR).
Rnds 1–2: K all sts.
Rnd 3: (SSK) 2 times, K4, (K2tog) 2 times, K16. (24 sts)
Rnds 4–5: K all sts.
Rnd 6: SSK, K4, K2tog, K3, (SSK) 2 times, K2, (K2tog) 2 times, K3. (18 sts)
Rnd 7: K all sts.
Rnd 8: SSK, K2, K2tog, K1, (SSK) 2 times, K2, (K2tog) 2 times, K1. (12 sts)

Position safety eyes (if using) 1"/2.5 cm from neckline and 1"/2.5 cm apart from each other at top; attach. Eyes can also be embroidered.
Rnd 9: K all sts.
Rnd 10: SSK, K2tog, K1, SSK, K2, K2tog, K1. (8 sts)

Stuff neck and head through opening. Cut yarn, and thread through remaining live sts; pull closed. Weave in loose ends. With a scrap of white yarn, embroider lines around the eyes. The nose can be embroidered with a scrap of pink, beige, or black yarn.

• Ears (make 2)

The ears are worked separately with color A and seamed to top of head. CO 4 sts onto 1 dpn; the ears are worked flat.

Row 1: P all sts.
Row 2: K all sts.
Row 3: P all sts.
Row 4: SSK, K2tog. (2 sts)
Row 5: P all sts.

Cut yarn, thread through remaining live sts, and pull closed. Weave in loose end on P side of work. Fold ear in half lengthwise with CO edge at the bottom and right sides together; stitch closed at bottom with CO tail, creating an indention in the center. Seam to head 4 sts behind eyes and about 4 sts apart from each other on the top.

• Feet (make 2)

With color A, CO 9 sts onto 3 dpns and join in the round. Knit all sts for 14 rounds. Cut yarn, thread through live sts, and pull closed. Weave in loose end. Stuff very lightly; flatten and seam CO edge

to the bottom of your squirrel with about 10 rows of the foot visible from the front.

• Tail

The tail is worked separately with color A and then seamed to body. CO 12 sts onto 3 dpns, join in the round.

Rnds 1–5: K all sts.
Row 6: K2, w&t.
Row 7: P4, w&t.
Row 8: K5, w&t.
Row 9: P6, w&t.
Row 10: K7, w&t.
Row 11: P8, w&t.
Row 12: K9, w&t.
Row 13: P19, w&t.
Row 14: K5 (EOR).
Rnd 15: (M1, K3) 4 times. (16 sts)
Rnds 16–19: K all sts.
Rnd 20: (M1, K4) 4 times. (20 sts)
Rnds 21–24: K all sts.
Rnd 25: (M1, K5) 4 times. (24 sts)
Rnds 26–37: K all sts.
Rnd 38: (M1, K6) 4 times. (28 sts)
Rnd 39: K all sts.
Row 40: K18, w&t.
Row 41: P8, w&t.
Row 42: K10, w&t.
Row 43: P12, w&t.

Row 44: K14, w&t.
Row 45: P16, w&t.
Row 46: K18, w&t.
Row 47: P20, w&t.
Row 48: K22, w&t.
Row 49: P24, w&t.
Row 50: K16, w&t.
Row 51: P8, w&t.
Row 52: K10, w&t.
Row 53: P12, w&t.
Row 54: K14, w&t.
Row 55: P16, w&t.
Row 56: K22 (EOR).
Rnd 57: K all sts.
Rnd 58: (K2, K2tog) 7 times. (21 sts)
Rnds 59–60: K all sts.
Rnd 61: (K1, K2tog) 7 times. (14 sts)
Rnds 62–63: K all sts.
Rnd 64: (K2tog) 7 times. (7 sts)
Rnd 65: K all sts.

Cut yarn, thread through remaining live sts, and pull closed. Weave in loose end.

Stuff tail; seam CO edge to bottom/center of body. Seam or tack tail to back of body about halfway up to hold in place.

Hands can be either sewn together or hot-glued to a nut or acorn on both sides.

GOLIATH FROG

* Sighted at Nyong river
– Cameroon, Africa

They sit and wait for prey on nearby rocks & logs.

Due to deforestation, these animals are endangered as their populations are decreasing.

Goliath frogs can still leap a distance of 10ft!

Longest of the frog species found on Earth and can grow up to 12.5 inches in length and weigh up to 7.2 lbs!

Their backs or dorsal sides are covered with green and the underside is yellow-orange

☆ Goliath Frogs are primarily nocturnal

Goliath Frog

SIZE

17"/43 cm long
7"/18 cm wide

YARN

Cascade 220 Superwash Merino, #3 to #4 light to medium weight, 100% superwash merino wool, 220 yd./200 m per 3.5 oz./100 g skein
- A suggestions: 37 Toasted Coconut; 18 Dark Olive (top side); 160 yd./146 m
- B: 44 Snap Dragon (bottom side); 130 yd./119 m

NEEDLES

US size 3/3.25 mm dpns
US size 3/3.25 mm straight needles

NOTIONS

18 mm green or yellow cat safety eyes
Darning needle
Stuffing

INSTRUCTIONS

• Bottom of Body

Work begins with mouth. With color B, CO 28 sts onto 1 straight needle.
Row 1: P all sts.
Row 2: K all sts.
Row 3: P all sts.
Row 4: K17, w&t.
Row 5: P6, w&t.
Row 6: K8, w&t.
Row 7: P10, w&t.
Row 8: K12, w&t.
Row 9: P14, w&t.
Row 10: K16, w&t.
Row 11: P18, w&t.
Row 12: K20, w&t.
Row 13: P22, w&t.
Row 14: K24, w&t.
Row 15: P26, w&t.
Row 16: K27 (EOR).
Row 17: P all sts.
Row 18: K all sts.
Row 19: P all sts.
Row 20: K all sts.

Row 21: P all sts.
Row 22: SSK, K24, K2tog. (26 sts)
Row 23: P all sts.
Row 24: SSK, K22, K2tog. (24 sts)
Row 25: P all sts.
Row 26: K1, M1L, K22, M1R, K1. (26 sts)
Row 27: P all sts.
Row 28: K all sts.
Row 29: P all sts.
Row 30: K1, M1L, K24, M1R, K1. (28 sts)
Rows 31–59: Work 29 rows stockinette stitch.
Row 60: SSK, K24, K2tog. (26 sts)
Row 61: P all sts.
Row 62: K all sts.
Row 63: P all sts.
Row 64: K all sts.
Row 65: P all sts.
Row 66: SSK, K22, K2tog. (24 sts)
Row 67: P all sts.
Row 68: K all sts.
Row 69: P all sts.
Row 70: K all sts.
Row 71: P all sts.
Row 72: SSK, K20, K2tog. (22 sts)
Row 73: P all sts.
Row 74: K all sts.
Row 75: P all sts.
Row 76: SSK, K18, K2tog. (20 sts)
Row 77: P all sts.
Row 78: K all sts.
Row 79: P all sts.
Row 80: (SSK) 2 times, K12, (K2tog) 2 times. (16 sts)
Row 81: P all sts.
Row 82: (SSK) 2 times, K8, (K2tog) 2 times. (12 sts)
Row 83: P all sts.
Row 84: (SSK) 2 times, K4, (K2tog) 2 times. (8 sts)
Row 85: P all sts.
Row 86: (SSK) 2 times, (K2tog) 2 times. (4 sts)
  Cast off P-wise. Cut yarn, thread through last st, and pull closed. Weave in loose ends.

• Top of Body

Work begins at mouth. With color A, CO 36 sts onto 1 straight needle.

Row 1: P all sts.
Row 2: K all sts.
Row 3: P all sts.
Row 4: K21, w&t.
Row 5: P6, w&t.
Row 6: K8, w&t.
Row 7: P10, w&t.
Row 8: K12, w&t.
Row 9: P14, w&t.
Row 10: K16, w&t.
Row 11: P18, w&t.
Row 12: K20, w&t.
Row 13: P22, w&t.
Row 14: K24, w&t.
Row 15: P26, w&t.
Row 16: K28, w&t.
Row 17: P30, w&t.
Row 18: K32, w&t.
Row 19: P34, w&t.
Row 20: K35 (EOR).
Row 21: P all sts.
Row 22: SSK, K32, K2tog. (34 sts)
Row 23: P all sts.
Row 24: SSK, K30, K2tog. (32 sts)
Row 25: P all sts.
Row 26: K1, M1L, K30, M1R, K1. (34 sts)
Row 27: P all sts.
Row 28: K all sts.
Row 29: P all sts.
Row 30: K1, M1L, K32, M1R, K1. (36 sts)
Row 31: P all sts.
Row 32: K all sts.
Row 33: P all sts.
Row 34: K1, M1L, K34, M1R, K1. (38 sts)
Row 35: P all sts.
Row 36: K all sts.
Row 37: P all sts.
Row 38: K1, M1L, K36, M1R, K1. (40 sts)
Row 39: P all sts.
Row 40: K all sts.
Row 41: P all sts.
Row 42: K1, M1L, K38, M1R, K1. (42 sts)
Row 43: P all sts.
Row 44: K all sts.
Row 45: P all sts.
Row 46: K1, M1L, K40, M1R, K1. (44 sts)
Rows 47–59: Work 13 rows stockinette stitch.

Row 60: (SSK) 2 times, K36, (K2tog) 2 times. (40 sts)
Row 61: P all sts.
Row 62: K all sts.
Row 63: P all sts.
Row 64: K all sts.
Row 65: P all sts.
Row 66: (SSK) 2 times, K32, (K2tog) 2 times. (36 sts)
Row 67: P all sts.
Row 68: K all sts.
Row 69: P all sts.
Row 70: K all sts.
Row 71: P all sts.
Row 72: (SSK) 2 times, K28, (K2tog) 2 times. (32 sts)
Row 73: P all sts.
Row 74: (SSK) 2 times, K24, (K2tog) 2 times. (28 sts)
Row 75: P all sts.
Row 76: (SSK) 2 times, K20, (K2tog) 2 times. (24 sts)
Row 77: P all sts.
Row 78: (SSK) 2 times, K16, (K2tog) 2 times. (20 sts)
Row 79: P all sts.
Row 80: (SSK) 2 times, K12, (K2tog) 2 times. (16 sts)
Row 81: P all sts.
Row 82: (SSK) 2 times, K8, (K2tog) 2 times. (12 sts)
Row 83: P all sts.
Row 84: (SSK) 2 times, K4, (K2tog) 2 times. (8 sts)
Row 85: P all sts.
Row 86: (SSK) 2 times, (K2tog) 2 times. (4 sts)

Cast off P-wise. Cut yarn, thread through last st, and pull closed. Weave in loose ends.

• Seaming

STEP 1: THE HEAD

The top and bottom pieces of the head are now seamed together. Place right sides together and line up the CO edges on each piece. Hold the two pieces so that the corners as well as the CO edges are aligned. The top piece will extend 4 sts beyond the bottom piece on each side, so it will need to be scrunched up a little in order to make the corners line up. This extra fabric is what creates the height on top of the head.

With a darning needle and a piece of color B yarn, begin 4 sts or about ¾" from the CO edge in the center of your frog's head. Make a running stitch going toward the outside and rounding out the corner as you reach it, gradually decreasing the width of the seam until you are about 15 sts or 3.5" from the center where you started. This seam will coincide with the wrapped sts from the short rows in the front. Start in the center again, and repeat going the opposite direction toward the other side.

STEP 2: THE 4 STS AT BOTTOM

Turn your frog so that right sides are facing out, and then seam the 4 cast-off sts at the bottom together.

STEP 3: THE SIDE SEAMS

Count 15 rows up from both sides of the seam in step 2; these will be the leg openings. Hold top and bottom pieces together and, beginning there, seam the two pieces together along the edges toward the head for 38 rows. This will leave openings for the arms that are 10 rows wide.

ARMS AND LEGS

Each of the 4 frog legs are worked flat using 2 dpns, the top pieces with color A and the bottom pieces with color B. For clarification in this pattern, the front legs will be called arms. Right and left refer to the frog's right and left. For ease in knitting, leave arms and legs unseamed and everything unstuffed until all 8 pieces are worked.

• Bottom Right Leg

Setup: Holding the frog belly-side up and with head pointed to the right, PU 16 sts with color B and 1 dpn along the bottom (color B) section of the right leg opening.

Row 1: P all sts.
Row 2: K all sts.
   Repeat last 2 rows 5 more times for a total of 12 rows worked in stockinette stitch.
Row 13: P all sts.
Row 14: SSK, K12, K2tog. (14 sts)
Row 15: P all sts.
Row 16: K all sts.
Row 17: P all sts.
Row 18: K12, K2tog. (13 sts)
Row 19: P all sts.
Row 20: K11, K2tog. (12 sts)
Row 21: P all sts.
Row 22: SSK, K8, K2tog. (10 sts)

Row 23: P all sts.
Row 24: SSK, K8. (9 sts)
Row 25: P all sts.
Row 26: K5, w&t.
Row 27: P5.
Row 28: K6, w&t.
Row 29: P6.
Row 30: K7, w&t.
Row 31: P7.
Row 32: K8, w&t.
Row 33: P8.
Row 34: SSK, K3, w&t. (8 sts)
Row 35: P4.
Row 36: K5, w&t.
Row 37: P5.
Row 38: SSK, K4, w&t. (7 sts)
Row 39: P5.
Row 40: K6, w&t.
Row 41: P6.
Row 42: K6, M1R, K1. (8 sts)
Row 43: P all sts.
Row 44: K all sts.

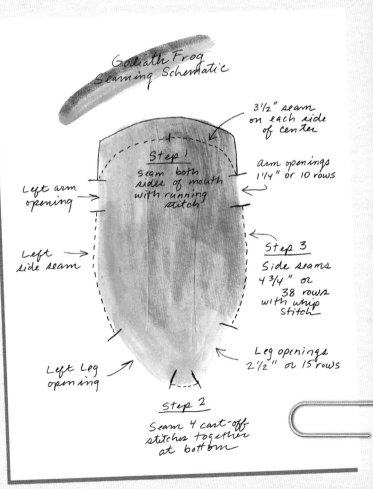

Goliath Frog
Seaming Schematic

3 1/2" seam on each side of center

Step 1
Seam both sides of mouth with running stitch

arm openings 1 1/4" or 10 rows

Left arm opening

Step 3
Side seams 4 3/4" or 38 rows with whip stitch

Left side seam

Leg openings 2 1/2" or 15 rows

Left Leg opening

step 2
Seam 4 cast-off stitches together at bottom

Row 45: P all sts.
Row 46: K all sts.
Row 47: P all sts.
Row 48: K6, K2tog. (7 sts)
Row 49: P all sts.
Row 50: K5, K2tog. (6 sts)
Row 51: P all sts.
Row 52: K4, K2tog. (5 sts)
Row 53: P all sts.
Row 54: K all sts.
Row 55: P all sts.
Row 56: K3, K2tog. (4 sts)
  Cut yarn; leave sts on dpn.

• Top Right Leg

Setup: Holding the frog right side up and with head pointed down, PU 18 sts with color A and 1 dpn along the top (color A) section of the right leg opening.
Row 1: P all sts.
Row 2: K all sts.
  Repeat last 2 rows 5 more times for a total of 12 rows worked in stockinette stitch.
Row 13: P all sts.
Row 14: SSK, K14, K2tog. (16 sts)
Row 15: P all sts.
Row 16: K all sts.
Row 17: P all sts.
Row 18: SSK, K14. (15 sts)
Row 19: P all sts.
Row 20: SSK, K13. (14 sts)
Row 21: P all sts.
Row 22: SSK, K10, K2tog. (12 sts)
Row 23: P all sts.
Row 24: K10, K2tog. (11 sts)
Row 25: P7, w&t.
Row 26: K7.
Row 27: P8, w&t.
Row 28: K8.
Row 29: P9, w&t.
Row 30: K9.
Row 31: P10, w&t.
Row 32: K10.
Row 33: P2tog, P5, w&t. (10 sts)
Row 34: K6.
Row 35: P7, w&t.
Row 36: K7.
Row 37: P2tog, P6, w&t. (9 sts)
Row 38: K7.
Row 39: P8, w&t.
Row 40: K8.

Row 41: P all sts.
Row 42: K1, M1L, K8. (10 sts)
Row 43: P all sts.
Row 44: K all sts.
Row 45: P all sts.
Row 46: K all sts.
Row 47: P all sts.
Row 48: SSK, K8. (9 sts)
Row 49: P all sts.
Row 50: SSK, K7. (8 sts)
Row 51: P all sts.
Row 52: SSK, K6. (7 sts)
Row 53: P all sts.
Row 54: K all sts.
Row 55: P all sts.
Row 56: SSK, K5. (6 sts)
  Do not cut working yarn. Arrange remaining sts onto 2 dpns. These will be joined in the round with the 4 sts from the bottom leg to work the foot.

• Right Foot

Feet are worked in the round with color A only.
Setup: K4 (the previous color B sts); (EOR).
Rnds 1–2: K all sts. (10 sts)
Row 3: K1, w&t.

Row 4: P2, w&t.
Row 5: K3, w&t.
Row 6: P4, w&t.
Row 7: K5, w&t.
Row 8: P6, w&t.
Row 9: K3 (EOR).
Rnds 10–11: K all sts.
Rnd 12: (K2, M1L, K1, M1R, K2) 2 times. (14 sts)
Rnds 13–15: K all sts.
Rnd 16: (K3, M1L, K1, M1R, K3) 2 times. (18 sts)
Rnds 17–19: K all sts.
Rnd 20: (K2, SSK, K1, K2tog, K2) 2 times. (14 sts)
Rnds 21–23: K all sts.
Rnd 24: (K1, SSK, K1, K2tog, K1) 2 times. (10 sts)
Rnds 25–27: K all sts.
Rnd 28: (K1, SSK, K2tog) 2 times. (6 sts)
   Cut yarn, thread through remaining live sts and pull closed. Weave in loose ends.

• Bottom Left Leg

Setup: Holding the frog belly-side up and with head pointed down, PU 16 sts with color B and 1 dpn along the bottom (color B) section of the left leg opening.
Row 1: P all sts.
Row 2: K all sts.
   Repeat last 2 rows 5 more times for a total of 12 rows worked in stockinette stitch.
Row 13: P all sts.
Row 14: SSK, K12, K2tog. (14 sts)
Row 15: P all sts.
Row 16: K all sts.
Row 17: P all sts.
Row 18: SSK, K12. (13 sts)
Row 19: P all sts.
Row 20: SSK, K11. (12 sts)
Row 21: P all sts.
Row 22: SSK, K8, K2tog. (10 sts)
Row 23: P all sts.
Row 24: K8, K2tog. (9 sts)
Row 25: P5, w&t.
Row 26: K5.
Row 27: P6, w&t.
Row 28: K6.
Row 29: P7, w&t.
Row 30: K7.
Row 31: P8, w&t.
Row 32: K8.
Row 33: P2tog, P3, w&t. (8 sts)
Row 34: K4.
Row 35: P5, w&t.

Row 36: K5.
Row 37: P2tog, P4, w&t. (7 sts)
Row 38: K5.
Row 39: P6, w&t.
Row 40: K6.
Row 41: P all sts.
Row 42: K1, M1L, K6. (8 sts)
Row 43: P all sts.
Row 44: K all sts.
Row 45: P all sts.
Row 46: K all sts.
Row 47: P all sts.
Row 48: SSK, K6. (7 sts)
Row 49: P all sts.
Row 50: SSK, K5. (6 sts)
Row 51: P all sts.
Row 52: SSK, K4. (5 sts)
Row 53: P all sts.
Row 54: K all sts.
Row 55: P all sts.
Row 56: SSK, K3. (4 sts)
   Cut yarn; leave sts on dpn.

• Top Left Leg

Setup: Holding the frog right side up and with head pointed to the right, PU 18 sts with color A and 1 dpn along the top (color A) section of the left leg opening.
Row 1: P all sts.
Row 2: K all sts.
   Repeat last 2 rows 5 more times for a total of 12 rows worked in stockinette stitch.
Row 13: P all sts.
Row 14: SSK, K14, K2tog. (16 sts)
Row 15: P all sts.
Row 16: K all sts.
Row 17: P all sts.
Row 18: K14, K2tog. (15 sts)
Row 19: P all sts.
Row 20: K13, K2tog. (14 sts)
Row 21: P all sts.
Row 22: SSK, K10, K2tog. (12 sts)
Row 23: P all sts.
Row 24: SSK, K10. (11 sts)
Row 25: P all sts.
Row 26: K7, w&t.
Row 27: P7.
Row 28: K8, w&t.
Row 29: P8.
Row 30: K9, w&t.
Row 31: P9.

Row 32: K10, w&t.
Row 33: P10.
Row 34: SSK, K5, w&t. (10 sts)
Row 35: P6.
Row 36: K7, w&t.
Row 37: P7.
Row 38: SSK, K6, w&t. (9 sts)
Row 39: P7.
Row 40: K8, w&t.
Row 41: P8.
Row 42: K8, M1R, K1. (10 sts)
Row 43: P all sts.
Row 44: K all sts.
Row 45: P all sts.
Row 46: K all sts.
Row 47: P all sts.
Row 48: K8, K2tog. (9 sts)
Row 49: P all sts.
Row 50: K7, K2tog. (8 sts)
Row 51: P all sts.
Row 52: K6, K2tog. (7 sts)
Row 53: P all sts.
Row 54: K all sts.
Row 55: P all sts.
Row 56: K5, K2tog. (6 sts)

Do not cut yarn. Arrange remaining sts onto 2 dpns. These will be joined in the round with the 4 sts from the bottom leg to work the foot.

• Left Foot

Worked the same as the right foot, except do not K4 first—go straight to round 1. The EOR will be in a different place than the right foot so that they will both point outward.

• Bottom Right Arm

Setup: Hold frog belly-side up with head pointed to the right. PU 10 sts along the bottom (color B) section of the right arm opening.
Row 1: P all sts. (10 sts)
Row 2: K all sts.
Row 3: P all sts.
Row 4: K all sts.
Row 5: P all sts.
Row 6: K all sts.
Row 7: P all sts.
Row 8: K all sts.
Row 9: P5, w&t.
Row 10: K5.
Row 11: P6, w&t.
Row 12: K6.

Row 13: P7, w&t.
Row 14: K7.
Row 15: P8, w&t.
Row 16: K8.
Row 17: P9, w&t.
Row 18: K9.
Row 19: P all sts.
Row 20: SSK, K6, K2tog. (8 sts)
Row 21: P all sts.
Row 22: K all sts.
Row 23: P all sts.
Row 24: K all sts.
Row 25: P all sts.
Row 26: K all sts.
Row 27: P all sts.
Row 28: SSK, K4, K2tog. (6 sts)
Row 29: P all sts.
Row 30: K all sts.
Row 31: P all sts.
Row 32: SSK, K2, K2tog. (4 sts)

Cast off P-wise. Cut yarn, thread through last st, and pull closed. Weave in loose ends.

• Top Right Arm

Setup: Hold frog right side up with head pointed to the left. PU 12 sts along the top (color A) section of the right arm opening.
Row 1: P all sts.
Row 2: K all sts.
Row 3: P all sts.
Row 4: K all sts.
Row 5: P all sts.
Row 6: K all sts.
Row 7: P all sts.
Row 8: K5, w&t.
Row 9: P5.
Row 10: K6, w&t.
Row 11: P6.
Row 12: K7, w&t.
Row 13: P7.
Row 14: K8, w&t.
Row 15: P8.
Row 16: K9, w&t.
Row 17: P9.
Row 18: SSK, K8, K2tog. (10 sts)
Row 19: P all sts.
Row 20: K all sts.
Row 21: P all sts.
Row 22: K all sts.
Row 23: P all sts.
Row 24: K all sts.

Row 25: P all sts.
Row 26: SSK, K6, K2tog. (8 sts)
Row 27: P all sts.
Row 28: K all sts.
Row 29: P all sts.
Row 30: K all sts.
Row 31: P all sts.

• Fingers

4 fingers are worked at the end of the arm tops with color A. The fingers are 2-st I-cords of varying lengths with a bobble at the end of each one.

BOBBLE

1. (Kfb) 2 times, turn work. (4 sts)
2. P4, turn work.
3. Slip 2, K2tog, (PSSO) 2 times.

1ST FINGER

K2, slip sts to the other side of dpn. Work 2 rows of a 2-st I-cord. Make Bobble. Cut yarn; use the loose end to further shape and define the bobble.

2ND FINGER

Rejoin working yarn at next st; K6, turn work, P6. K2, slip sts to the other side of dpn. Work 5 rows of a 2-st I-cord. Make Bobble. Cut yarn; use the loose end to further shape and define the bobble.

3RD FINGER

Rejoin working yarn at next st. K2, slip sts to the other side of dpn. Work 2 rows of a 2-st I-cord. Make Bobble. Cut yarn; use the loose end to further shape and define the bobble.

4TH FINGER

Rejoin working yarn at next st. Make Bobble. Cut yarn; use the loose end to further shape and define the bobble.

Weave in loose ends. Fingers can be worked the same on second hand or mirrored.

• Bottom Left Arm

Setup: Hold frog belly-side up with head pointing to the left. PU 10 sts along the bottom (color B) section of the left arm opening.

Row 1: P all sts. (10 sts)
Row 2: K all sts.
Row 3: P all sts.
Row 4: K all sts.

Row 5: P all sts.
Row 6: K all sts.
Row 7: P all sts.
Row 8: K5, w&t.
Row 9: P5.
Row 10: K6, w&t.
Row 11: P6.
Row 12: K7, w&t.
Row 13: P7.
Row 14: K8, w&t.
Row 15: P8.
Row 16: K9, w&t.
Row 17: P9.
Row 18: K all sts.
Row 19: P all sts.
Row 20: SSK, K6, K2tog. (8 sts)
Row 21: P all sts.
Row 22: K all sts.
Row 23: P all sts.
Row 24: K all sts.
Row 25: P all sts.
Row 26: K all sts.
Row 27: P all sts.
Row 28: SSK, K4, K2tog. (6 sts)
Row 29: P all sts.
Row 30: K all sts.
Row 31: P all sts.
Row 32: SSK, K2, K2tog. (4 sts)

Cast off P-wise. Cut yarn, thread through last st, and pull closed. Weave in loose ends.

• Top Left Arm

Setup: Hold frog right side up with head pointing to the right. PU 12 sts along the top (color A) section of the left arm opening.

Row 1: P all sts. (12 sts)
Row 2: K all sts.
Row 3: P all sts.
Row 4: K all sts.
Row 5: P all sts.
Row 6: K all sts.
Row 7: P all sts.
Row 8: K all sts.
Row 9: P5, w&t.
Row 10: K5.
Row 11: P6, w&t.
Row 12: K6.
Row 13: P7, w&t.
Row 14: K7.
Row 15: P8, w&t.
Row 16: K8.
Row 17: P9, w&t.
Row 18: K9.
Row 19: P all sts.
Row 20: SSK, K8, K2tog. (10 sts)
Row 21: P all sts.
Row 22: K all sts.
Row 23: P all sts.
Row 24: K all sts.
Row 25: P all sts.
Row 26: K all sts.
Row 27: P all sts.
Row 28: SSK, K6, K2tog. (8 sts)
Row 29: P all sts.
Row 30: K all sts.
Row 31: P all sts.

Work fingers in either the same or reverse order.

• Seaming and Stuffing

The arms and legs are seamed along the outside edges with a whipstitch. Seaming and stuffing in this order makes it easier:

1. Stuff body through legs
2. Seam one leg, stuffing just before closing
3. Repeat with the second leg
4. Seam an arm, stuffing just before closing
5. Repeat with second arm

The cast-off edge of the bottom arm is seamed to the top arm just below fingers.

• Eye Pockets (make 2 the same)

A small pocket is now created and seamed to the head with the open side down; the safety eye is attached to the front of it.

With color A, CO 8 sts to 1 dpn and work the following rows back and forth.

Row 1: P all sts.
Row 2: K all sts.
Row 3: P all sts.
Row 4: K5, w&t.
Row 5: P2, w&t.
Row 6: K3, w&t.
Row 7: P4, w&t.
Row 8: K5, w&t.
Row 9: P6, w&t.
Row 10: K7 (EOR).

Cast off P-wise. Flatten and stitch corners together, shaping it into a pocket. Position safety eyes in the center of the cast-off side and even with the bottom edge; place back of safety eye on the post inside of pocket.

Seam open end of pockets to top of head about 14 rows back from center of mouth and 6 sts apart from each other on top, turning to face slightly outward.

BROWN RAT

x Sighted in back of building, Prospect Heights Brooklyn, New York

They live in large colonies made up of smaller social units (or 'clans')

They dig extensive burrows that may be used for generations.

They are intelligent and highly adaptable animals, and have lived alongside humans for millennia

very smart!

Brown rats have grey-brown fur and a long, scaly tail, which is used to help balance.

Brown rats spend a lot of their time washing and grooming, although they often live around trash & dumpsters - They are fastidiously clean.

Excellent swimmers and divers, agile climbers, & occasionally climb trees.

Brown Rat

SIZE

8"/20 cm long, not counting tail
3"/7.5 cm wide

YARN

Cascade Aereo, #4 medium weight, 47% merino wool/31% baby alpaca/22% nylon, 240 yd./220 m per 3.5 oz./100 g skein

- A suggestions: 05 Doeskin Heather; 06 Walnut Heather (head and body); 80 yd./73 m

Cascade 220, #4 medium weight, 100% Peruvian Highland wool, 220 yd./200 m per 3.5 oz./100 g skein

- B suggestions: 8021 Beige; 8011 Aspen Heather; 1033 Nectarine (tail); 5 yd./4.5 m
- C suggestions: 1033 Nectarine; 9681 Crabapple; 4192 Soft Pink (inside ears, feet); 10 yd./9 m

NEEDLES

US size 5/3.75 mm dpns
US size 3/3.25 mm dpns

NOTIONS

6 mm round black safety eyes (optional)
Darning needle
Stuffing
White sewing thread (whiskers)

INSTRUCTIONS

• Body and Tail

Work begins at top/center of neckline. With color A and larger-size needles, CO 22 sts onto 3 dpns. Join in the round by slipping the first CO st onto the 3rd needle and then pulling the 2nd stitch (formerly the last st) over it and off the needle; 21 sts remain.

Rnd 1: K all sts.
Rnd 2: M1R, K20, M1L, K1. (23 sts)
Rnds 3–5: K all sts.
Rnd 6: M1R, K22, M1L, K1. (25 sts)
Rnds 7–9: K all sts.
Rnd 10: M1R, K24, M1L, K1. (27 sts)
Rnds 11–13: K all sts.
Rnd 14: M1R, K26, M1L, K1. (29 sts)
Rnds 15–17: K all sts.
Rnd 18: M1R, K1, M1R, K26, (M1L, K1) 2 times. (33 sts)
Rnds 19–21: K all sts.
Rnd 22: M1R, K1, M1R, K30, (M1L, K1) 2 times. (37 sts)
Rnds 23–25: K all sts.
Rnd 26: M1R, K1, M1R, K34, (M1L, K1) 2 times. (41 sts)
Rnds 27–29: K all sts.

Rnd 30: (K4, K2tog) 3 times, K5, (SSK, K4) 3 times. (35 sts)

Rnds 31–32: K all sts.

Rnd 33: (K3, K2tog) 3 times, K5, (SSK, K3) 3 times. (29 sts)

Rnds 34–35: K all sts.

Rnd 36: (K2, K2tog) 3 times, K5, (SSK, K2) 3 times. (23 sts)

Rnds 37–38: K all sts.

Rnd 39: (K1, K2tog) 3 times, K5, (SSK, K1) 3 times. (17 sts)

Rnds 40–41: K all sts.

Rnd 42: (K2tog) 3 times, K5, (SSK) 3 times. (11 sts)

Rnds 43–44: K all sts.

Rnd 45: (K2tog) 2 times, K3, (SSK) 2 times. (7 sts)

Rnd 46: K2tog, K3, SSK. (5 sts)

K2; cut color A. Move the 2 sts just worked down to opposite side of the dpn; then slip the 3 remaining sts (beginning with the last st in the round) onto this working dpn. All 5 sts should now be on the same dpn, with the cut piece of color A coming from the bottom stitch.

• Tail

An I-cord is now worked to make the tail. Switch to smaller-size dpns, and join color B at first st on needle. Work rows 2–47 as an I-cord, pulling the working yarn up from the bottom stitch.

Rnd 1: K all sts. (5 sts)

Rows 2–7: Work 5-stitch I-cord.

Row 8: K2tog, K3. (4 sts)

Rows 9–28: Work 4-stitch I-cord.

Row 29: K2tog, K2. (3 sts)

Rows 30–40: Work 3-stitch I-cord.

Row 41: K2tog, K1. (2 sts)

Rows 42–47: Work 2-stitch I-cord.

Cut yarn, thread through 2 remaining sts, and pull closed. Stuff body, accentuating the curve in the back and flattening the underside. Weave in all loose ends.

• Head

Sts are now picked up in the original CO sts to begin the head. With color A and larger-size dpns,

begin in first CO st (top/center of back), PU 21 sts, 1 in each CO st; join sts in the round.

Row 1: K5, w&t.

Row 2: P10, w&t.

Row 3: K11, w&t.

Row 4: P12, w&t.

Row 5: K13, w&t.

Row 6: P14, w&t.

Row 7: K7 (EOR).

Rnd 8: (K1, K2tog, K5, SSK) 2 times, K1. (17 sts)

Rnd 9: K all sts.

Rnd 10: (K1, K2tog, K3, SSK) 2 times, K1. (13 sts)

Rnd 11: K all sts.

Rnd 12: K4, SSK, K1, K2tog, K4. (11 sts)

Rnd 13: K all sts.

Safety eyes are attached now about 8 rows from neckline and 3 sts apart from each other.

Rnd 14: K3, SSK, K1, K2tog, K3. (9 sts)

Rnd 15: K all sts.

Rnd 16: K2, SSK, K1, K2tog, K2. (7 sts)

Cut yarn. Stuff head, adding more stuffing to body if needed. Thread end of yarn through remaining live sts, and pull closed. Weave in loose ends.

• Ears (make 2)

The ears are worked separately in 2 pieces, seamed together, and then seamed to head. With color A and larger-size dpns, CO 4 sts onto 1 dpn, leaving a tail of a few inches for seaming, and work the following rows back and forth.

Row 1: P all sts.

Row 2: K all sts.

Row 3: P all sts.

Row 4: SSK, K2tog. (2 sts)

Cut yarn, thread through last 2 sts, and pull closed. Weave in loose end on P side.

Repeat all instructions a second time with color C and smaller-size dpns.

Hold knit sides of the two pieces together with CO edges aligned; whipstitch around all edges with the color A CO tail, leaving the CO edges open. Turn right-side out. The color A side will be slightly larger than the color B side and show around the edges from the front. Ear is then flattened and can be pressed with a hot iron, if desired. It will make them flatter, but this step is not necessary. Fold in half lengthwise (pink side in) and take a stitch or two at CO edge to hold

closed and create a hollow inside the ear. Make another ear exactly the same and sew to head with the open part facing forward and outward about 4 rows behind the eyes and 4 sts apart from each other.

• Legs (make 4)

With color A, CO 16 sts onto 3 of the larger-size dpns. Join in the round by slipping the first CO st onto the 3rd needle and then pulling the 2nd stitch (formerly the last st) over it and off the needle; 15 sts remain.

Rnd 1: K all sts.
Rnd 2: (K2tog, K3) 3 times. (12 sts)
Rnd 3: K all sts.
Rnd 4: (K2tog, K2) 3 times. (9 sts)
Rnd 5: K all sts.
Rnd 6: (K2tog, K1) 3 times. (6 sts)

Cut color A; join color C and switch to the smaller-size dpns, both of which are used for the remainder of the leg.

Rnd 7: K all sts.
Rnd 8: (K2tog) 3 times, all on the same dpn. (3 sts)

Work 3 rows of an I-cord and then cut yarn. Thread through live sts and pull closed. Weave in all loose ends. Legs are not stuffed.

Seam the CO edge of the front legs to body about 5 rows from neckline and 2 sts apart from each other.

The upper parts of the back legs are flattened and seamed to body, slightly pointing outward about 8 rows from start of tail and touching each other in the middle.

Embroider the eyes (if not using safety eyes) with black yarn and the nose with color C. Add whiskers with sewing thread.

~ AMERICAN BISON ~

Sighted at Custer State Park, South Dakota

Bison have shaggy, dark coats in the winter, and lighter weight, lighter-colored coats in the summer.

Once Roamed North America in vast heards.

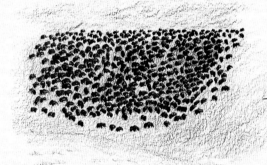

Nearly became extinct by commercial hunting and slaughter in the 19th century.

The bison is considered a sacred animal and religious symbol among many Native American tribes.

Both male and female bison have short, curved horns.

They are herbivores, grazing on grasses of the North American prairies.

Brown-headed cowbirds have a long-standing relationship with bison, having followed the herds on the Great Plains for centuries, feed on insects flushed from the grass.

American Bison

SIZE

12"/30.5 cm long
6"/15 cm wide

YARN

Cascade Aereo, #4 medium weight, 47% merino wool/31% baby alpaca/22% nylon, 240 yd./220 m per 3.5 oz./100 g skein
- A suggestions: 08 Camel; 05 Doeskin Heather (front of body and front legs); 60 yd./55 m
- B suggestions: 07 Mocha Heather; 06 Walnut Heather (back of body, back legs, head); 60 yd./55 m

NEEDLES

US size 5/3.75 mm dpns
US size 8/5.0 mm dpns

NOTIONS

Darning needle
Scrap of light-colored worsted weight yarn for horns
Stitch markers
Stuffing

Note: WiP = work in pattern: The stitch pattern used for the front body, front legs, and top of head is the basic seed stitch: Row 1: (K1, P1); Row 2: (P1, K1). This will change a bit once increases, decreases, and short rows are worked, but if you always remember to K the P stitches and P the K stitches, it will turn out fine.

INSTRUCTIONS

• Front of Body/Front Legs

Work begins with the right front leg and progresses across the back to the left front leg. With color A held double, CO 9 sts onto 3 larger-size dpns and join in the round. Rows 1–8 are worked in the round; the center part of the back is worked flat and then switched back to in-the-round knitting for the left leg.

Rnds 1–2: K all sts. (9 sts)
Rnds 3–8: WiP.
Turn work after round 8 and each of the rows below:
Row 9 (WS): WiP.
Row 10 (RS): Kfb, WiP to end. (10 sts)
Row 11: WiP.
Row 12: Kfb, WiP to end. (11 sts)
Add removable st markers on each edge of the RS. WiP flat for a total of 37 more rows, or 18 P bumps along the outside edge of your work from the point of the marker, finishing after a WS row.

Short rows are now worked to form the hump on the bison's back. Work as written below, turning your work after each row. The 2nd st from the end on the right side will be wrapped a total of 7 times.

Hump Rows:
Row 1: WiP for 9 sts, w&t.
Row 2: WiP for 7 sts, w&t.
Row 3: WiP for 6 sts, w&t.
Row 4: WiP for 6 sts, w&t.
Row 5: WiP for 5 sts, w&t.
Row 6: WiP for 5 sts, w&t.
Row 7: WiP for 4 sts, w&t.
Row 8: WiP for 4 sts, w&t.
Row 9: WiP for 3 sts, w&t.
Row 10: WiP for 3 sts, w&t.
Row 11: WiP for 2 sts, w&t.
Row 12: WiP for 2 sts, w&t.
Row 13: WiP for 1 st, w&t.
Row 14: WiP for 1 st, w&t.
Row 15: W&t.
Row 16: K1, P1.
WiP flat for 37 more rows, or until there are 18 P bumps along the outside edge of your work after the hump row; finishing after a WS row. Add

removable st markers on each edge of the RS; continue below:

Row 1 (RS): SSK, WiP to end. (10 sts)
Row 2: WiP.
Row 3: SSK, WiP to end. (9 sts)
Row 4: WiP.
Row 5: WiP.

Arrange sts onto 3 dpns, join in the round and work the rounds below:

Rnds 6–10: WiP.
Rnds 11–12: K all sts.

Cast off.

• Back of Body

Sts are now picked up along the edge of your work to begin the back of the body. Switch to smaller-size dpns and one strand of color B yarn. With RS facing and hump pointed down, PU 55 sts with 3 dpns (19-18-18) along the edge between the st markers: PU 3 sts for every 2 P bumps—one under a P bump, a second under a P bump, and the third in between the last P bump and before the next one. Repeat until there are 19 sts on your 1st dpn, 18 sts on your 2nd, and 18

on your 3rd. Check to make sure the 2nd dpn is centered with 9 sts on each side of the hump.

Join sts in the round by slipping the 1st st to the end of the round on the 3rd dpn and then pulling the 2nd st over it and off the needle (54 sts). Tighten the first and last sts together.

Rnds 1–5: K all sts.
Rnd 6: K25, SSK, K2tog, K25. (52 sts)
Rnds 7–9: K all sts.
Rnd 10: K24, SSK, K2tog, K24. (50 sts)
Rnds 11–13: K all sts.
Rnd 14: K23, SSK, K2tog, K23. (48 sts)
Rnds 15–17: K all sts.
Rnd 18: K2tog, K1, K2tog, K17, SSK, K2tog, K17, SSK, K1, SSK. (42 sts)
Rnds 19–21: K all sts.
Rnd 22: K2tog, K1, K2tog, K14, SSK, K2tog, K14, SSK, K1, SSK. (36 sts)
Rnds 23–25: K all sts.

• Left Back Leg

Row 1: K22, w&t.
Row 2: P8, w&t.
Row 3: K9, w&t.
Row 4: P10, w&t.
Row 5: K11, w&t.
Row 6: P12, w&t.
Row 7: K13, w&t.
Row 8: P14, w&t.
Row 9: K25.
Rnd 10: K all sts.

Sts are now divided in half to finish working the legs. K18 sts all on one dpn, and place remaining 18 sts on a piece of scrap yarn. The following section is a set of short rows to shape the left buttock. With WS facing, continue below, turning your work after each row:

Row 1: Slip 1, P1, w&t, K2.
Row 2: Slip 1, P2, w&t, K3.
Row 3: Slip 1, P3, w&t, K4.
Row 4: Slip 1, P4, w&t, K5.
Row 5: Slip 1, P5, w&t, K6.
Row 6: Slip 1, P6, w&t, K7.
Row 7: Slip 1, P7, w&t, K8.
Row 8: Slip 1, P8, w&t, K9.

Arrange sts on 3 dpns, join in the round, and continue with the left leg:

Rnd 1: K all sts.
Rnd 2: K2tog, K14, SSK. (16 sts)
Rnd 3: K all sts.
Rnd 4: K2tog, K12, SSK. (14 sts)

Rnd 5: K all sts.

Rnd 6: K2tog, K10, SSK. (12 sts)

Rnd 7: K all sts.

Rnd 8: K2tog, K8, SSK. (10 sts)

Rnds 9–10: K all sts.

The next round includes a set of short rows to create the bend in the leg. These short rows (on both legs) will be worked on both sides of the EOR. Be careful to maintain the EOR by either a st marker or a break between 1st and 3rd dpns:

Rnd 11: K9, w&t, P2, w&t, K3, w&t, P4, w&t, K5, w&t, P6, w&t, K5 (EOR).

Rnd 12: K2tog, K6, SSK. (8 sts)

Rnds 13–24: K all sts.

Rnd 25: K1, M1, K2, M1, K5. (10 sts)

Rnd 26: K4, w&t, P4, w&t (EOR).

Rnd 27: Cast off all sts, leaving a tail of several inches.

Stuff hoof; then, with loose end, close the bottom of the hoof by sewing a few sts across in several directions.

• Right Back Leg

Place 18 sts from scrap yarn onto 1 dpn. With RS facing, rejoin yarn at 1st st and begin to shape the right buttock. Turn your work after each row:

Row 1: K2, w&t, P2.

Row 2: Slip 1, K2, w&t, P3.

Row 3: Slip 1, K3, w&t, P4.

Row 4: Slip 1, K4, w&t, P5.

Row 5: Slip 1, K5, w&t, P6.

Row 6: Slip 1, K6, w&t, P7.

Row 7: Slip 1, K7, w&t, P8.

Row 8: Slip 1, K8, w&t, P9.

Row 9: Slip 1, K17.

Arrange sts on 3 dpns; join in the round.

Rnd 1: K all sts.

Rnd 2: K2tog, K14, SSK. (16 sts)

Rnd 3: K all sts.

Rnd 4: K2tog, K12, SSK. (14 sts)

Rnd 5: K all sts.

Rnd 6: K2tog, K10, SSK. (12 sts)

Rnd 7: K all sts.

Rnd 8: K2tog, K8, SSK. (10 sts)

Rnds 9–10: K all sts.

Rnd 11: K3, w&t, P2, w&t, K3, w&t, P4, w&t, K5, w&t, P6, w&t, K1 (EOR).

Rnd 12: K2tog, K6, SSK. (8 sts)

Rnds 13–24: K all sts.

Rnd 25: K4, M1, K2, M1, K2. (10 sts)

Rnd 26: K7, w&t, P4 w&t, K7.

Cast off all sts, leaving a tail of several inches.

Stuff and close hoof the same as above.

Turn the rear of your bison inside out, and, holding right sides of buttocks together, seam closed.

• Front Hooves

Sts are now picked up around the bottom edge of front legs to add hooves. Work the rounds below with smaller dpns and one strand of color B yarn.

Setup: Beginning in the center back of front leg, PU 10 sts with 3 dpns.

Rnd 1: K all sts.

Rnd 2: (K2tog, K3) 2 times. (8 sts)

Rnd 3: K all sts.

Rnd 4: K3, M1, K2, M1, K3. (10 sts)

Rnd 5: K7, w&t, P4, w&t, K7 (EOR).

Cast off all sts, leaving a tail of a few inches.

Stuff hoof and close the same way as for the back hooves.

• Head

Sts are now picked up along the opposite edge to begin the head. With RS facing and hump pointed upward, PU 37 sts with 3 dpns (15-8-14) between the st markers. 1 st is picked up under every P bump. Check to make sure the 2nd dpn is centered with 4 sts on each side of the hump.

Join sts in the round by slipping the 1st st to the end of the round on the 3rd dpn and then

Row 7: K8.

Repeat last 2 rows 6 times for a total of 14 rows worked in stockinette stitch, and then cast off.

Stuff head as fully as possible (stuffing will be coming out of opening). Hold flap just worked over stuffing; bottom edge should hang about ½"/1.25 cm below the opening at bottom. With a darning needle and one strand of color B yarn, seam one side, folding bottom corners and bottom edge under when you get to them.

• Flap between Front Legs

A small piece of fabric is worked from one leg to the other in order to join the front legs. With larger dpns and color A held double, PU 10 sts along one side of the opening; then work the following rows back and forth:

Row 1: P all sts.

Row 2: K6, w&t, P2, w&t, K3, w&t, P4, w&t, K7.

Cast off all sts on WS.

Stuff every part of your bison fully, using a dpn from the outside to shift stuffing down into all 4 hooves and legs. Make sure there is enough stuffing in the middle section to maintain the hump and curve of the back. If there's not enough, the bison will appear to have a swayback.

After stuffing, seam the flap between front legs to the other side and on both ends.

• Horns

With scrap of light-colored yarn and smaller needles, PU 5 sts in a cluster exactly where head flap begins. Join sts in the round.

Rnds 1–4: K all sts.

Rnd 5: K2tog, K3. (4 sts)

Rnd 6: K2tog, K2. (3 sts)

Rnd 7: K2tog, K1. (2 sts)

Cut yarn, thread through last 2 sts, and pull closed. Weave in loose ends. Repeat in same place on the other side of head.

• Tail

The tail is a 4- to 5-inch piece of color B yarn, with the bottom frayed a bit. Attach to center of rear end.

pulling the 2nd st over it and off the needle (36 sts). Tighten the first and last sts together.

Rnd 1: K all sts.

Rnd 2: K2tog, K12, (Kfb) 8 times, K12, SSK. (42 sts)

Rnd 3: K13, (P1, K1) 8 times, K13.

Rnd 4: K2tog, K11, WiP16, K11, SSK. (40 sts)

Rnd 5: K12, WiP16, K12.

Rnd 6: K2tog, K10, WiP16, K10, SSK. (38 sts)

Rnd 7: K11, WiP16, K11.

Rnd 8: K2tog, K9, WiP16, K9, SSK. (36 sts)

The next round contains short rows in the middle to shape the head and change direction of the work:

Rnd 9: K10, WiP12, w&t, WiP8, w&t, WiP9, w&t, WiP10, w&t, WiP11, w&t, WiP12, w&t, WiP14, K10 (EOR).

Rnd 10: Cast off first 12 sts, WiP12, cast off last 12 sts. (12 sts)

With RS facing, rejoin two strands of color B yarn at first st and work the following rows flat, turning your work after each one:

Row 1: K4, WiP4, K4.

Row 2: P4, WiP4, P4.

Row 3: SSK, K3, WiP2, K3, K2tog. (10 sts)

Row 4: P4, WiP2, P4.

Row 5: SSK, K2, WiP2, K2, K2tog. (8 sts)

Row 6: P8.

The young are born in litters ranging from one to eleven and remain with their mothers for only 4-7 weeks before heading out on their own. ♥

when they feel alarmed or intimidated they will curl up into a spiny ball to protect its vulnerable stomach.

EUROPEAN HEDGEHOG

*Sighted at Regents Park - London, England

Hedgehogs have about 5,000 spines. Each spine lasts about a year then drops outs and a replacement grows.

Since 2002, the UK has lost around 30-50% of it hedgehog population due to habitat loss.

European hedgehogs hibernate throughout the winter.

They are nocturnal, traveling 1-2 kilometers per night in search of food.

European Hedgehog

SIZE

10"/25.5 cm long
6"/15 cm wide

YARN

Cascade Aereo Duo (2 strands held double)
or Cascade Aereo (2 colors held together),
#4 medium weight, 47% merino wool/31%
baby alpaca/22% nylon, 240 yd./220 m per
3.5 oz./100 g skein
- A suggestions: 205 Caramel Mocha; 206 Sable
  (body); 100 yd./91 m

Cascade Aereo, #4 medium weight, 47% merino
wool/31% baby alpaca/22% nylon, 240 yd./220 m
per 3.5 oz./100 g skein
- B suggestions: 04 Ecru; 08 Camel (belly and
  face); 30 yd./27.5 m

Cascade 220, #4 medium weight, 100%
Peruvian Highland wool, 220 yd./200 m per
3.5 oz./100 g skein
- C suggestions: 9477 Tutu; 8622 Camel (legs);
  5 yd./4.5 m

NEEDLES

US size 8/5.0 mm straight needles
US size 5/3.75 mm dpns
US size 3/3.25 mm dpns

NOTIONS

9 mm black safety eyes
Darning needle
Scrap of black yarn for embroidering nose
Stuffing

Note: If you are unfamiliar with the loop stitch
(abbreviated lp), there are many YouTube videos
you can watch. Some of them have slight
variations, but the overall finished look is the
same. I also recommend knitting a small swatch
of loop stitch for practice before getting started
on the pattern.

INSTRUCTIONS

• lp (Loop Stitch)

1. Knit into stitch but do not slip off needle.
2. Bring yarn to front between the needles.
3. Place thumb on the yarn and pull the yarn
   up over your thumb and back between the
   needles.
4. Keeping the yarn wrapped around your thumb,
   knit into the front of the same stitch, this time
   slipping it off the needle.
5. Remove your thumb, and you will have a loop
   hanging between two stitches.
6. Pull the 2nd st on the right needle over the last
   st and off the needle.

• K2toglp

1. Knit into next 2 sts but do not slip off left
   needle.
2. Bring yarn to front between the needles.
3. Place thumb on the yarn and pull the yarn
   up over your thumb and back between the
   needles.
4. Keeping the yarn wrapped around your thumb,
   knit into the front of the same stitch, this time
   slipping it off the needle.
5. Remove your thumb, and you will have a loop
   hanging between two stitches.
6. Pull the 2nd st on the right needle over the last
   st and off the needle.

• ssklp

1. Work an ssk, but leave the single st created on
   the left needle.
2. Bring yarn to front between the needles.
3. Place thumb on the yarn and pull the yarn
   up over your thumb and back between the
   needles.
4. Keeping the yarn wrapped around your thumb,
   knit into the front of the same stitch, this time
   slipping it off the needle.
5. Remove your thumb, and you will have a loop
   hanging between two stitches.
6. Pull the 2nd st on the right needle over the last
   st and off the needle.

• Body

Work begins with top of head. Use double strand of Cascade Aereo Duo or 2 strands of Cascade Aereo in 2 different colors and size 8/5.0 mm straight needles. The body is worked flat. CO 6 sts onto 1 needle.

Row 1: P all sts.
Row 2: Lp all sts. (6 sts)
Row 3: P all sts.
Row 4: Lp1, M1R, lp to last st, M1L, lp1. (8 sts)
Row 5: P all sts.

Repeat rows 4 and 5 until a total of 30 sts is reached.

Short rows are now worked over just some of the sts to shape the back.

Row 1: Lp1, M1R, lp18, w&t. (31 sts)
Row 2: P8, w&t.
Row 3: Lp9, w&t.
Row 4: P10, w&t.

Row 5: Lp11, w&t.
Row 6: P12, w&t.
Row 7: Lp13, w&t.
Row 8: P14, w&t.
Row 9: Lp15, w&t.
Row 10: P16, w&t.
Row 11: Lp17, w&t.
Row 12: P18, w&t.
Row 13: Lp19, w&t.
Row 14: P20, w&t.
Row 15: Lp21, w&t.
Row 16: P22, w&t.
Row 17: Lp25, M1L, lp1. (32 sts)
Row 18: P all sts.

Knitting over all of the sts is now resumed.

Row 19: (K2toglp) 8 times, (SSKlp) 8 times. (16 sts)
Row 20: P all sts.
Row 21: (K2toglp) 4 times, (SSKlp) 4 times. (8 sts)
Row 22: P all sts.

Row 23: (K2toglp) 2 times, (SSKlp) 2 times. (4 sts)
Row 24: P all sts.
Row 25: K2toglp, SSKlp. (2 sts)

Cut yarn, thread through last 2 sts, and pull closed.

• Belly

Work begins at neckline. The belly piece is worked flat with a single strand of color B and two size 5/3.75 mm dpns. With color B, CO 14 sts onto 1 dpn.

Row 1: Slip 1, P to end.
Row 2: Slip 1, K to end.
Row 3: Slip 1, P to end.
Row 4: Slip 1, M1R, K to last st, M1L, K1. (16 sts)

Repeat rows 1–4 until there are a total of 22 sts, ending after an increase row.

Beginning with the next P row, work 17 rows of straight stockinette st, slipping the first st of every row; then continue below.

Row 5: SSK, K to last 2 sts, K2tog. (20 sts)
Row 6: Slip 1, P to end.
Row 7: Slip 1, K to end.
Row 8: Slip 1, P to end.

Repeat rows 5–8 until there are a total of 16 sts; then work row 5 one more time. (14 sts)

Cast off all sts on P side.

Turn body piece upside down and position belly piece with K side facing outward on top of the opening. CO edge of belly piece should begin where body was increased to 10 sts (6th row). The first 5 rows of the body that extend beyond the belly will become the top of the head.

The belly piece will need to lay concave down inside of body in order to fit properly and create the appropriate shape when stuffed. Before seaming, it may be helpful to pin the center of the CO edge to the center of body row 6 and the center of the CO edge to the center of the last row of the body piece so that the two ends are straight across when finished seaming. It may also be helpful to pin in several places along the sides.

Seam belly piece to body with color B and a whipstitch along edge of work just below the first loop on every row. CO edge is left open for working head.

After seaming the two pieces together, stuff the body; use a dpn from the outside to distribute stuffing evenly.

• Head

Sts for the head are picked up along front edge and in the CO sts of the belly piece. Use a single strand of color B and size 5/3.75 mm dpns.

With RS facing, begin at center of front edge of top of head. Check to make sure this is aligned with the center of the belly piece. Since the body doesn't knit up in perfect symmetry, this may be off slightly. If so, adjust where to begin picking up sts for the head based on center of belly. Note: When picking up the first and last 12 sts, it will be necessary to include some "in between" sts to reach the right number.

- 1st dpn: PU 12 sts along the edge below the loops from front/center of top of head down to belly piece
- 2nd dpn: PU 14 sts in CO sts of belly
- 3rd dpn: PU 12 sts along the edge below the loops from belly piece to front/center of top of head

Join sts in the round. (38 sts total)

Rnds 1–5: K all sts.
Rnd 6: (K2tog) 4 times, K5, (SSK) 3 times, (K2tog) 3 times, K5, (SSK) 4 times. (24 sts)
Rnds 7–8: K all sts.

Attach safety eyes (if using) now. They should be halfway between first row of color B and edge of current work, with 6–8 sts in between. Then stuff neck and head.

Rnd 9: (K2tog) 4 times, (SSK) 2 times, (K2tog) 2 times, (SSK) 4 times. (12 sts)

Rnds 10–13: K all sts.

Rnd 14: K4, SSK, K2tog, K4. (10 sts)

Rnd 15: K all sts.

Rnd 16: K3, SSK, K2tog, K3. (8 sts)

Cut yarn, and thread through remaining live sts. Add more stuffing to the nose before pulling closed.

Embroider nose with scrap of black yarn.

Face shaping: Flatten forehead and push first row of loops up and away from face. Encourage nose to bend slightly upward. If the face is angled downward, use a dpn to push stuffing from belly up toward the front and into the bottom of the neck and head—doing so will bring the face up.

Duplicate stitching can be worked on the face if sts are overstretched.

• Ears (make 2 the same)

Ears are worked separately and seamed to head. With a single strand of either color A or color B, CO 8 sts onto 3 size 5/3.75 mm dpns and join in the round. K 3 rounds.

Cut yarn, thread through live sts, and pull closed. Weave in loose end. Ear is left unstuffed and flattened. Seam CO edge to head with the CO tail.

• Legs (make 2 the same)

Legs are worked in the round with color C and size 3/3.25 mm dpns. CO 8 sts onto 3 dpns and join sts in the round. K all sts for 12 rounds. Cut yarn, thread through live sts, and pull closed. Weave in loose end. Stuff and seam to belly midway between neckline and end of body, with 6 sts in between them. The last 3–4 rounds can be bent forward for the foot.

EASTERN COTTONTAIL RABBIT

* Sighted at Occone Greenway, Milledgeville Georgia

a female can produce a litter of up to 8 kits (or kittens) every 30 days.

Cottontails are prey for a variety of predators — coyotes, owls, hawks, foxes, skunks, raccoons, snakes, weasels, opossums, cats, and dogs.

They use camouflage and deception to hide their nests.

Cottontails range in color from a reddish brown to grey, but ALL have the trademark white cotton-ball tail.

They usually freeze at the first sight of danger and run as a last resort, but when they do run, it's up to 18 miles per hour, and in a zig-zag pattern to confuse predators.

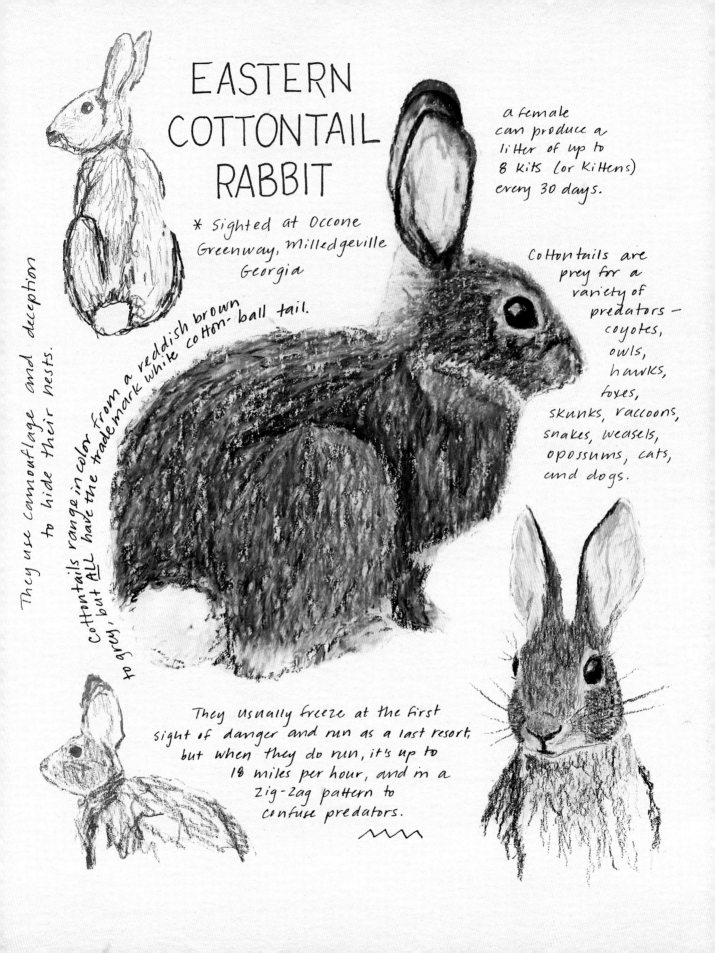

Eastern Cottontail Rabbit

SIZE

18"/45.5 cm long
5"/12.5 cm wide

YARN

Cascade Aereo, #4 medium weight, 47% merino wool/31% baby alpaca/22% nylon, 240 yd./220 m per 3.5 oz./100 g skein
- A suggestions: 05 Doeskin Heather; 06 Walnut Heather (everything but underside of tail); 130 yd./119 m
- B: 04 Ecru (underside of tail); 2 yd./2 m

NEEDLES

US size 5/3.75 mm straight needles
US size 5/3.75 mm dpns

NOTIONS

Darning needle
Stitch marker
Stuffing
Wire for ear support (optional)

• Chest

With color A, CO 24 sts onto 1 straight needle; the chest is worked flat.
Row 1: P all sts.
Row 2: K all sts.
Row 3: P all sts.
Row 4: K1, M1, K22, M1, K1. (26 sts)
Row 5: P all sts.
Row 6: K all sts.
Row 7: P all sts.
Row 8: K1, M1, K24, M1, K1. (28 sts)
Row 9: P all sts.
Row 10: K all sts.
Row 11: P all sts.
Row 12: K1, M1, K26, M1, K1. (30 sts)
Row 13: P all sts.
Row 14: K all sts.
Row 15: P all sts.
Row 16: K1, M1, K28, M1, K1. (32 sts)

Row 17: P all sts.
Row 18: K all sts.
Row 19: P all sts.
Row 20: K all sts.
Row 21: P all sts.
Row 22: K all sts.

• Front Left Leg

Slip last 16 sts onto 3 dpns and join them in the round. Place remaining 16 sts on a piece of scrap yarn. K 1 round, and then K2. Sts are now arranged on 2 dpns as follows: sts 3–10 on one, and sts 11–16 plus 1–2 on the other. The following 4 rows are worked back and forth on sts 11–2 and will shape the back of the elbow.

Row 1: Slip 1, P7.
Row 2: Slip 1, K7.
Row 3: Slip 1, P7.
Row 4: Slip 1, K7.

Arrange those 8 sts on 2 dpns with right sides facing each other. Work a 3-needle bind-off; cut yarn, and thread through last st. Turn work right-side out.

Rejoin working yarn at 1st st on needle, and PU sts for the leg.

- 1st dpn: K2tog, K2, place a marker, K2, SSK
- 2nd dpn: PU 5 sts along outside top edge of elbow
- 3rd dpn: PU 5 sts along inside top edge of elbow (16 sts)
  K3 to reach marker (EOR).

Rnd 1: K all sts.
Rnd 2: K3, K2tog, K6, SSK, K3. (14 sts)
Rnd 3: K all sts.
Rnd 4: K3, K2tog, K4, SSK, K3. (12 sts)
Rnd 5: K all sts.
Rnd 6: K3, K2tog, K2, SSK, K3. (10 sts)
Rnds 7–14: K all sts.
Rnd 15: K3, K2tog, SSK, K3. (8 sts)
Rnds 16–23: K all sts.
Rnd 24: K1, M1, K6, M1, K1. (10 sts)
Rnds 25–26: K all sts.
Rnd 27: K2, w&t, P4, w&t, K2.
Rnd 28: K3, w&t, P6, w&t, K3.
Rnd 29: K4, w&t, P8, w&t, K4.

Cut yarn, thread through remaining live sts, and pull closed. Use loose end to stitch small hole on bottom of paw closed.

• Front Right Leg

Place 16 sts from scrap yarn onto 1 dpn and with RS facing, K all sts. Arrange sts onto 3 dpns and join in the round.

K6, and then (as with the other leg) arrange sts on 2 dpns as follows: sts 1–6 plus 15–16 on one, and sts 7–14 on the other. Repeat all instructions as for the left elbow and leg.

• Body

Seam together top 4 rows of the chest to create the neck opening. Sts are now picked up for the body.
- 1st dpn: PU 18 sts along right edge of work from neck seam to elbow
- 2nd dpn: PU 8 sts along bottom edge of work from elbow to elbow
- 3rd dpn: PU 18 sts along left edge of work from elbow to neck seam (44 sts)

Rnd 1: K all sts.
Rnd 2: K21, M1, K2, M1, K21. (46 sts)
Rnd 3: K all sts.
Rnd 4: K22, M1, K2, M1, K22. (48 sts)
Rnd 5: K all sts.
Rnd 6: K23, M1, K2, M1, K23. (50 sts)
Rnds 7–11: K all sts.
Rnd 12: M1, K23, K2tog, SSK, K22, M1, K1.
Rnds 13–15: K all sts.
Rnd 16: M1, K23, K2tog, SSK, K22, M1, K1.
Rnds 17–19: K all sts.
Rnd 20: M1, K23, K2tog, SSK, K22, M1, K1.
Rnds 21–23: K all sts.
Rnd 24: M1, K23, K2tog, SSK, K22, M1, K1.
Rnds 25–27: K all sts.
Rnd 28: M1, K23, K2tog, SSK, K22, M1, K1.
Rnds 29–31: K all sts.
Rnd 32: M1, K23, K2tog, SSK, K22, M1, K1.
Rnd 33: K all sts.
Rnd 34: K23, K2tog, SSK, K23. (48 sts)
Rnd 35: K all sts.
Rnd 36: M1, K22, K2tog, SSK, K21, M1, K1.
Rnd 37: K all sts.
Rnd 38: K22, K2tog, SSK, K22. (46 sts)
Rnd 39: K all sts.
Rnd 40: K21, K2tog, SSK, K21. (44 sts)
Rnd 41: K all sts.
Rnd 42: K20, K2tog, SSK, K20. (42 sts)
Rnd 43: K all sts.
Rnd 44: K19, K2tog, SSK, K19. (40 sts)
Rnd 45: K8, w&t, P16, w&t, K8.
Rnd 46: K10, w&t, P20, w&t, K10.

• Back Right Leg

K20; place the remaining 20 on scrap yarn. CO 16 new sts to the end of the 20 sts on needles (EOR); arrange sts on 3 dpns and join in the round. (36 sts)

Rnd 1: K all sts.
Rnd 2: (SSK) 2 times, K28, (K2tog) 2 times. (32 sts)
Rnds 3–4: K all sts.
Rnd 5: (SSK) 2 times, K24, (K2tog) 2 times. (28 sts)
Rnds 6–7: K all sts.
Rnd 8: (SSK) 2 times, K20, (K2tog) 2 times. (24 sts)
Rnds 9–10: K all sts.
Rnd 11: (SSK) 2 times, K16, (K2tog) 2 times. (20 sts)
Rnds 12–13: K all sts.
Rnd 14: (SSK) 2 times, K12, (K2tog) 2 times. (16 sts)
Rnds 15–16: K all sts.

Work the following round exactly as written; multiple short rows are included within:
Rnd 17: K10, w&t, P4, w&t, K5, w&t, P6, w&t, K11.
Rnd 18: SSK, K12, K2tog. (14 sts)
Rnd 19: K all sts.
Rnd 20: SSK, K10, K2tog. (12 sts)
Rnd 21: K all sts.
Rnd 22: SSK, K8, K2tog. (10 sts)
Rnds 23–24: K all sts.
Rnd 25: SSK, K6, K2tog. (8 sts)
Rnds 26–28: K all sts.

K4; turn work. The beginning of the ankle is worked the same as the elbow.
Rnd 1: Slip 1, P7.
Rnd 2: Slip 1, K7.
Rnd 3: Slip 1, P7.
Rnd 4: Slip 1, K7.

Rnd 5: Slip 1, P7.

Arrange sts on 2 dpns with right sides facing each other, and then work a 3-needle bind-off; cut yarn, and thread through last st. Turn work right-side out. Beginning on the leg side of the opening, PU 10 sts with 3 dpns around the top edge.

The rounds below will begin with the first picked-up st.

Rnds 1–3: K all sts. (10 sts)

Rnd 4: K3, M1, K4, M1, K3. (12 sts)

Rnds 5–10: K all sts.

Rnd 11: K1, M1, K10, M1, K1. (14 sts)

Rnds 12–15: K all sts.

Rnd 16: K2, w&t, P4, w&t, K2.

Rnd 17: K3, w&t, P6, w&t, K3.

Rnd 18: K4, w&t, P8, w&t, K4.

Cut yarn; thread through remaining live sts, and pull closed. Use loose end to stitch small hole on bottom of paw closed.

• Back Left Leg

Place 20 sts from scrap yarn onto 2 dpns. With RS facing, rejoin yarn at first st; K20. CO 16 new sts to the end (EOR); arrange sts on 3 dpns; join in the round. (36 sts)

Rnd 1: K all sts.

Rnd 2: K14, (K2tog) 2 times, (SSK) 2 times, K14. (32 sts)

Rnds 3–4: K all sts.

Rnd 5: K12, (K2tog) 2 times, (SSK) 2 times, K12. (28 sts)

Rnds 6–7: K all sts.

Rnd 8: K10, (K2tog) 2 times, (SSK) 2 times, K10. (24 sts)

Rnds 9–10: K all sts.

Rnd 11: K8, (K2tog) 2 times, (SSK) 2 times, K8. (20 sts)

Rnds 12–13: K all sts.

Rnd 14: K6, (K2tog) 2 times, (SSK) 2 times, K6. (16 sts)

Rnds 15–16: K all sts.

Rnd 17: K2, w&t, P4, w&t, K2.

Rnd 18: K3, w&t, P6, w&t, K3.

Rnd 19: K6, K2tog, SSK, K6. (14 sts)

Rnd 20: K all sts.

Rnd 21: K5, K2tog, SSK, K5. (12 sts)

Rnd 22: K all sts.

Rnd 23: K4, K2tog, SSK, K4. (10 sts)

Rnds 24–25: K all sts.

Rnd 26: K3, K2tog, SSK, K3. (8 sts)

Rnds 27–29: K all sts.

Turn work; the left ankle and foot are worked the same as the right.

Rnd 1: Slip 1, P7.
Rnd 2: Slip 1, K7.
Rnd 3: Slip 1, P7.
Rnd 4: Slip 1, K7.
Rnd 5: Slip 1, P7.

Arrange sts on 2 dpns with right sides facing each other, and then work a 3-needle bind-off; cut yarn, and thread through last st. Turn work right-side out. Beginning on the leg side of the opening, PU 10 sts with 3 dpns around the top edge.

The rounds below will begin with the first picked-up st.
Rnds 1–3: K all sts. (10 sts)
Rnd 4: K3, M1, K4, M1, K3. (12 sts)
Rnds 5–10: K all sts.
Rnd 11: K1, M1, K10, M1, K1. (14 sts)
Rnds 12–15: K all sts.
Rnd 16: K2, w&t, P4, w&t, K2.
Rnd 17: K3, w&t, P6, w&t, K3.

• Back of Head

With RS facing, count 6 sts to the right of the first CO st in your rabbit's neck. Beginning there and working to the left, PU 1 st in every CO st until you reach the center; then, with a 2nd dpn, PU 6 more sts on the left side of the center stitch (12 sts). Work 8 rows of stockinette st, beginning with a P row and ending with a K row. Sts can be arranged all on 1 dpn after a few rows.

• Ears

The ears are formed from the live sts at the back of the head. Slip the last 6 sts onto 3 dpns and join in the round. Place the remaining 6 sts on a piece of scrap yarn.
Rnd 1: K all sts.
Rnd 2: (K1, M1, K1) 3 times. (9 sts)
Rnds 3–4: K all sts.
Rnd 5: (K1, M1, K2) 3 times. (12 sts)
Rnds 6–9: K all sts.
Rnd 10: (K2, M1, K2) 3 times. (15 sts)
Rnds 11–14: K all sts.
Rnd 15: (K2, M1, K3) 3 times. (18 sts)
Rnds 16–20: K all sts.
Rnd 21: K2tog, K14, SSK. (16 sts)
Rnd 22: K all sts.
Rnd 23: K2tog, K12, SSK. (14 sts)
Rnd 24: K all sts.
Rnd 25: K2tog, K10, SSK. (12 sts)
Rnd 26: K all sts.

Rnd 27: K2tog, K8, SSK. (10 sts)
Rnd 28: K all sts.

Cut yarn, thread through live sts, and pull closed. Place 6 sts from scrap yarn onto 1 dpn. With RS facing, K6. Arrange sts on 3 dpns and join in the round. Repeat rounds 2–28. Manipulate ears to curve inward around the decreases.

• Head

Sts are picked up on the bottom of the ears, along the edges of the back of the head, and in the original CO sts to form the head. I recommend that you work with a set of 5 dpns for this section.

With RS of rabbit facing you but on the inside of your work, begin picking up sts between the ears and work to the left.

- **1st dpn:** PU 1 st between the ears, 2 on the bottom of left ear, 6 along the edge of the back of head and 1 in the original CO sts
- **2nd dpn:** PU 6 sts in the original CO sts from back of head to front/center of neck
- **3rd dpn:** PU 6 sts in the original CO sts from front/center of neck to back of head
- **4th dpn:** PU 1 in the original CO sts, 6 along the edge of the back of head, 2 on the bottom of the ear, and 1 between the ears (32 sts)

Rnd 1: K all sts.

Rnd 2: K10, (M1, K1) 4 times, K4, (K1, M1) 4 times, K10. (40 sts)

Rnd 3: K all sts.

Rnd 4: K4, SSK, K2tog, K2, (M1, K1) 4 times, K12, (K1, M1) 4 times, K2, SSK, K2tog, K4. (44 sts)

Rnd 5: K all sts.

Rnd 6: K3, SSK, K2tog, K30, SSK, K2tog, K3. (40 sts)

Rnd 7: K all sts.

Rnd 8: K2, SSK, K2tog, K28, SSK, K2tog, K2. (36 sts)

Rnd 9: K all sts.

Rnd 10: K1, SSK, K2tog, K26, SSK, K2tog, K1. (32 sts)

Rnd 11: K all sts.

Rnd 12: K1, SSK, K2tog, K22, SSK, K2tog, K1. (28 sts)

Rnd 13: K all sts.

Rnd 14: K1, SSK, K2tog, K18, SSK, K2tog, K1. (24 sts)

Rnd 15: K all sts.

Rnd 16: K1, SSK, K2tog, K5, K2tog, SSK, K5, SSK, K2tog, K1. (18 sts)

Rnd 17: K1, SSK, K2tog, K2, K2tog, SSK, K2, SSK, K2tog, K1. (12 sts)

Rnd 18: K1, SSK, K2tog, K2, SSK, K2tog, K1. (8 sts)

Rnd 19: K1, K2tog, K2, SSK, K1. (6 sts)

Cut yarn, thread through remaining live sts, and pull closed, but do not weave in or cut loose end. After stuffing your rabbit's head, insert darning needle below the nose and out the top of head to pull final stitch downward and create nose.

• Tail

Sts are picked up around the top of the opening between legs to begin the tail. It is made with 2 colors using the Fair Isle method of colorwork in which the yarn not being used is loosely carried behind the working yarn. Gradually decrease the number of color A sts and replace with color B as you work. The number of color A and color B sts worked is up to the knitter.

With RS facing, begin to PU sts on the left side of the opening, 5 sts down. The first st picked up will be the first st in the round.

- 1st dpn: PU 5 sts along the left side (3 color B; 2 color A)
- 2nd dpn: PU 4 sts across the top (color A)
- 3rd dpn: PU 5 sts along the right side (2 color A; 3 color B) (14 sts); EOR
  Join sts in the round.

Rnds 1–2: K all sts.

Rnd 3: K3, w&t, P6, w&t, K3.

Rnd 4: K4, w&t, P8, w&t, K4.

Rnds 5–7: K all sts.

Rnd 8: K5, SSK, K2tog, K5. (12 sts)

Rnd 9: K4, SSK, K2tog, K4. (10 sts)

Rnd 10: K3, SSK, K2tog, K3. (8 sts)

Rnd 11: K2, SSK, K2tog, K2. (6 sts)

Cut yarn, thread through remaining live sts, and pull closed. Stuff the base of the tail very loosely; the top of it should be left unstuffed.

Brush color B section gently with a wire pet brush to create a cottontail.

• Finishing

Stuff your rabbit loosely to moderately throughout, maintaining the curves of the body. Use a dpn from the outside to shift stuffing around body and to move it into legs and feet.

After stuffing, seam the hole between legs closed with color A.

To make front arms extend outward instead of down, shift stuffing into the elbows. To bring back legs closer together, shift stuffing up into rear end.

The ears will naturally fall backward a little; the degree will vary depending on where you picked up the sts for the head and the weight of your yarn. Wire can be added to keep them straight up.

Eyes are embroidered.

WESTERN MEADOWLARK

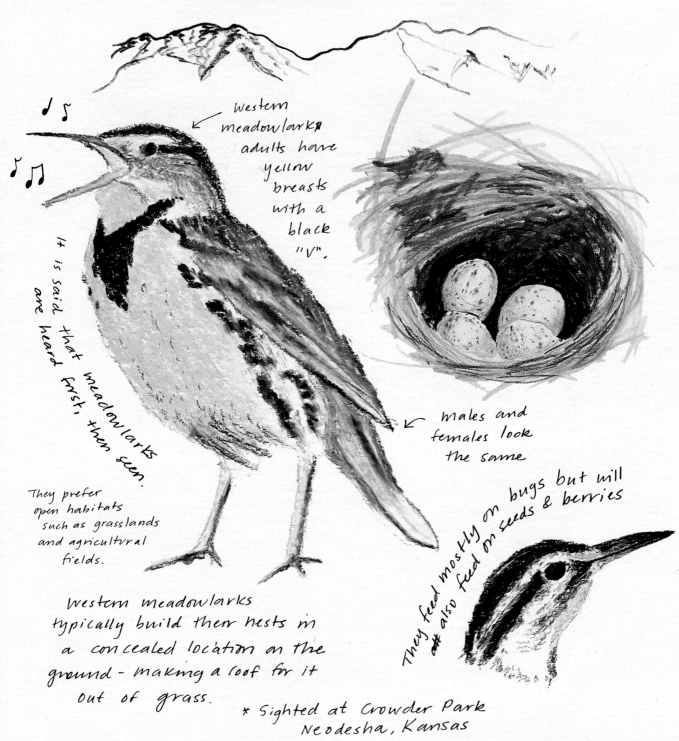

Western meadowlarks adults have yellow breasts with a black "V".

It is said that meadowlarks are heard first, then seen.

They prefer open habitats such as grasslands and agricultural fields.

Western meadowlarks typically build their nests in a concealed location on the ground - making a roof for it out of grass.

males and females look the same

They feed mostly on bugs but will also feed on seeds & berries

* Sighted at Crowder Park Neodesha, Kansas

Western Meadowlark

SIZE

7"/18 cm long
3.5"/9 cm wide

YARN

Cascade 220, #4 medium weight, 100% Peruvian Highland wool, 220 yd./200 m per 3.5 oz./100 g skein
- A: 8010 Natural (body); 20 yd./18 m
- B: 9463B Gold (breast, bottom of head); 10 yd./9 m
- C: 2441 River Rock (wings, top of head); 30 yd./27.5 m
- D: 8686 Brown (stripes on head, embroidery on body); 10 yd./9 m
- E: 8555 Black (embroidery on breast, eyes); 3 yd./2.75 m

NEEDLES

US size 3/3.25 mm dpns

NOTIONS

Darning needle
Stuffing

INSTRUCTIONS

• Body

Work begins at neckline. Body is worked flat at first with colors A and B using the intarsia method of colorwork. Begin by preparing a second ball of color A (8–10 yards) and CO 24 sts onto 1 dpn in the following colors and amounts:

Color A: CO 9
Color B: CO 6
Color A: CO 9 (24 sts)

When changing colors on any row, be sure to bring the new color over the old one to prevent a gap from forming between them.

Row 1 and all odd rows through 11 are purled using the same color as the preceding K row.
Row 2: Color A: K9; Color B: K6; Color A: K9.
Row 4: Color A: Kfb, K8. (10 sts); Color B: M1R, K6, M1L (8 sts); Color A: K8, Kfb (10 sts).
Row 6: Color A: Kfb, K9 (11 sts); Color B: M1R, K8, M1L (10 sts); Color A: K9, Kfb (11 sts).
Row 8: Color A: Kfb, K10 (12 sts); Color B: M1R, K10, M1L (12 sts); Color A: K10, Kfb (12 sts).
Row 10: Color A: K12; Color B: K12; Color A: K12.

Short rows in the following section create the rounded breast; continue using intarsia and maintaining all colors as they are in row 11.
Row 12: K23, w&t.
Row 13: P10, w&t.
Row 14: K12, w&t.
Row 15: P14, w&t.
Row 16: K16, w&t.
Row 17: P18, w&t.
Row 18: K20, w&t.
Row 19: P22, w&t.
Row 20: K24, w&t.
Row 21: P26, w&t.
Row 22: K28, w&t.
Row 23: P30, w&t.
Row 24: K33 (EOR).

Knitting all sts on each row is now resumed.
Row 25 and all odd rows 27–31: P all sts using the same color as the previous K row.
Row 26: Color A: K12; Color B: K2tog, K8, SSK (10 sts); Color A: K12.

Row 28: Color A: K12; Color B: K2tog, K6, SSK (8 sts); Color A: K12.

Row 30: Color A: K12; Color B: K2tog, K4, SSK (6 sts); Color A: K12.

Row 32: Color A: K12; Color B: K2tog, K2, SSK (4 sts); Color A: K12.

Cut color B and the first ball of color A; all rows for the remainder of the body are worked with 1 color only.

Row 33: P all sts. (28 sts)

Row 34: K all sts.

Row 35: P all sts.

Row 36: K11, SSK, K2, K2tog, K11. (26 sts)

Arrange sts on 3 dpns; the remainder of the body is worked in the round.

Rnd 37 and all odd rounds 39–55: K all sts.

Rnd 38: K10, SSK, K2, K2tog, K10. (24 sts)

Rnd 40: K9, SSK, K2, K2tog, K9. (22 sts)

Cut color A after round 41; join color C.

Rnd 42: K8, SSK, K2, K2tog, K8. (20 sts)

Rnd 44: K7, SSK, K2, K2tog, K7. (18 sts)

Rnd 46: K6, SSK, K2, K2tog, K6. (16 sts)

Rnd 48: K5, SSK, K2, K2tog, K5. (14 sts)

Rnd 50: K4, SSK, K2, K2tog, K4. (12 sts)

Rnd 52: K3, SSK, K2, K2tog, K3. (10 sts)

Rnd 54: K2, SSK, K2, K2tog, K2. (8 sts)

Rnd 56: K1, SSK, K2, K2tog, K1. (6 sts)

Cut yarn, thread through remaining live sts, and pull closed. Weave in loose ends.

Seam the flat section (rows 1–36) together with color A. Stuff body, rounding out the chest. The color C section at the end of the tail should only be stuffed halfway. The half at the end should be left unstuffed and flattened. To prevent stuffing from entering the end of the tail, a few small sts can be made in the middle of it with color C.

• Top of Head

Sts are picked up in the original CO sts to begin the head, which is worked in 2 pieces (top and bottom). To create the stripes, the top of the head is worked with the stranded method of colorwork, wherein the unused color is carried loosely behind the color that is being knitted.

With RS facing, begin on the right side of the head where the color A sts meet the color B sts and work to the left; a total of 18 sts are picked up on each side of the back/center of neck as follows:

- 1st dpn: Color C: PU 4; Color D: PU 1; Color C: PU 1; Color D: PU 2; Color C: PU 1

- 2nd dpn: Color C: PU 1; Color D: PU 2; Color C: PU 1; Color D: PU 1; Color C: PU 4

Row 1: P all sts the same color as they were picked up.

Placing all sts on 1 dpn may make knitting easier from this point forward. Short rows now create the curve in the head and change direction of the work. Continue using the same color for each st as you work the short rows.

Row 2: K12, w&t.

Row 3: P6, w&t.

Row 4: K7, w&t.

Row 5: P8, w&t.

Row 6: K9, w&t.

Row 7: P10, w&t.

Row 8: K14 (EOR).

Knitting all sts on each row is now resumed. Cut color D and continue with color C only.

Row 9: P all sts.

Row 10: (SSK, K1) 3 times, (K1, K2tog) 3 times. (12 sts)

Row 11: P all sts.

Row 12: (SSK, K1) 2 times, (K1, K2tog) 2 times. (8 sts)

Finished with top of head. Leave remaining live sts on dpn; do not cut color C.

• Bottom of Head

With color B, 1 dpn, and RS facing, PU 6 sts in the original color B CO sts from the right side of the breast to the left.

Row 1: P all sts.
Row 2: K all sts.
Row 3: P all sts.
Row 4: SSK, K2, K2tog. (4 sts)
Row 5: P all sts.
Row 6: SSK, K2tog. (2 sts)
Cut color B.

• Beak

Arrange all live sts from the top and bottom onto 3 dpns and join in the round (10 sts). The beak is worked in the round with color C only. K 2 sts remaining from the bottom of the head (EOR).
Rnd 1: K all sts.
Rnd 2: (SSK) 2 times, (K2tog) 2 times, K2. (6 sts)
Rnd 3: K all sts.
Rnd 4: SSK, K2tog, K2. (4 sts)
Rnd 5: K 4 all on 1 dpn.
Slip sts to the other side of dpn and work final 2 rows as an I-cord.
Row 6: K all sts.
Row 7: SSK, K2tog through the back loop. (2 sts)
Cut yarn, thread through last 2 sts, and pull closed. Weave in loose ends.

Stuff head; seam top to bottom on sides with color B. More stuffing can be added if needed before finishing the second seam.

• Wings (make 2 the same)

The wings are worked separately and seamed to the body afterward. After a few short rows to shape the beginning, they are worked in the round. With color C, CO 11 sts to 1 dpn and work rows 1–10 back and forth.
Row 1: P all sts.
Row 2: K7, w&t.
Row 3: P3, w&t.
Row 4: K4, w&t.
Row 5: P5, w&t.
Row 6: K6, w&t.
Row 7: P7, w&t.
Row 8: K8, w&t.
Row 9: P9, w&t.
Row 10: K10 (EOR).

Arrange the sts on 2 dpns with 5 on one and 6 on the other. With RS facing, sts are now picked up around the edge of work beginning at the previous EOR where the working yarn is coming from.

PU 11 sts with 2 dpns around the edge of work (new EOR); place a st marker here. Join sts in the round.

Rnds 1–2: K all sts. (22 sts)

Rnd 3: (K1, M1R, K9, M1L, K1) 2 times. (26 sts)

Rnds 4–13: K all sts.

Rnd 14: (K1, K2tog, K7, SSK, K1) 2 times. (22 sts)

Rnds 15–17: K all sts.

Rnd 18: (K1, K2tog, K5, SSK, K1) 2 times. (18 sts)

Rnds 19–21: K all sts.

Rnd 22: (K1, K2tog, K3, SSK, K1) 2 times. (14 sts)

Rnds 23–25: K all sts.

Rnd 26: (K1, K2tog, K1, SSK, K1) 2 times. (10 sts)

Rnds 27–29: K all sts.

Rnd 30: (K2tog, K1, SSK) 2 times. (6 sts)

Rnds 31–33: K all sts.

Cut yarn, thread through remaining live sts, and pull closed. Wings are left unstuffed and flattened with increases/decreases along the edges. Weave in loose ends.

Position wings on body with top edge running just to one side of the seam in the back/center of bird. The 2 wings should meet at the seam in the back. Seam to body with color C around all sides, except for about 1 inch in the back at the tip of the wing.

• Finishing

Use color D to embroider several small lines running horizontally (if your bird were standing) along the color A section below the wings.

The wings themselves are also embroidered with color D. Pictured are 3 vertical lines at a slight angle, but they can be embroidered any way you like.

The characteristic marking on the breast of the western meadowlark is embroidered with color E.

The eyes are also embroidered with color E.

TIMBER WOLF

* Sighted at Great Slave Lake - Yellowknife Northwest Territories, Canada

Timber wolves are carnivorous and feed on muskie oxen, bison, elk, moose, wild boar and caribou, eating up to 20 lbs. per meal.

Packs of wolves don't stay in one place and are known to travel as far as 12 mi. per day.

Timber wolves howl to communicate with other members of the ~~pake~~ pack.

nocturnal

Timber Wolf

SIZE

16"/40.5 cm long
4"/10 cm wide

YARN

Cascade Aereo, #4 medium weight, 47% merino wool/31% baby alpaca/22% nylon, 240 yd./220 m per 3.5 oz./100 g skein
- A suggestions: 02 Charcoal; 03 Silver; 05 Doeskin Heather (all but chest); 150 yd./137 m
- B: 04 Ecru (chest); 20 yd./18 m

NEEDLES

US size 8/5.0 straight needles
US size 5/3.75 mm dpns
US size 8/5.0 mm dpns

NOTIONS

Darning needle
Stitch marker (optional)
Straight sticks, dpns, or wire for stabilizing legs (optional)
Stuffing

INSTRUCTIONS

• Chest

Work begins in a straight line across the chest. Prepare 2 balls of color A (with yarn doubled) and 1 ball of color B (with yarn doubled). If desired, 2 different color As can be used to create a more realistic, multicolored look. All 3 balls should be around 10–12 yards in length. The chest section is worked using the intarsia method of colorwork, with color B in the center.

CO a total of 28 sts onto one size 8/5.0 mm straight needle as follows: 8 color A, 12 color B, 8 color A; work the following rows back and forth. Always bring the new color over the old one when switching colors to prevent a gap from forming between them. Color B stitch count will be decreased by 2 on all even rows after row 5.

Row 1: Color A: P8; Color B: P12; Color A: P8.
Row 2: Color A: K8; Color B: K12; Color A: K8.
Row 3: Color A: P8; Color B: P12; Color A: P8.
Row 4: Color A: K8; Color B: K12; Color A: K8.
Row 5: Color A: P8; Color B: P12; Color A: P8.
Row 6: Color A: SSK, K7; Color B: K10 (10 sts); Color A: K7, K2tog.
Row 7: Color A: P8; Color B: P10; Color A: P8.
Row 8: Color A: SSK, K7; Color B: K8 (8 sts); Color A: K7, K2tog.
Row 9: Color A: P8; Color B: P8; Color A: P8.
Row 10: Color A: SSK, K7; Color B: K6 (6 sts); Color A: K7, K2tog.
Row 11: Color A: P8; Color B: P6; Color A: P8.
Row 12: Color A: SSK, K7; Color B: K4 (4 sts); Color A: K7, K2tog.
Row 13: Color A: P8; Color B: P4; Color A: P8.
Row 14: Color A: SSK, K7; Color B: K2 (2 sts); Color A: K7, K2tog.
Row 15: Color A: P8; Color B: P2; Color A: P8.
Row 16: Color A: SSK, K14, K2tog. (16 sts)
Row 17: Color A: P16.

• Front Legs and Paws

Cut all strands of yarn. Switch to smaller-size dpns and one strand of color A yarn.

Setup: K8, place 8 on scrap yarn. Arrange first 8 sts on 3 dpns, CO 2 new sts to end of round, place a st marker or arrange sts with a break in the needles here to indicate EOR. CO 2 new sts to working needle, K10 (12 sts); EOR.
Rnds 1–5: K all sts.
Rnd 6: K2tog, K8, SSK. (10 sts)
Rnds 7–9: K all sts.
Rnd 10: K2tog, K6, SSK. (8 sts)
Rnds 11–32: K all sts.
Rnd 33: K2, (M1, K1) 4 times, K2. (12 sts)
Rnds 34–37: K all sts.

Rows 38–40 are short rows worked back and forth over just some of the sts; turn your work after each one.

Row 38: K8, w&t.
Row 39: P4, w&t.
Row 40: K8 (EOR).

Cut yarn, thread through live sts, and pull closed.

Place 8 sts from scrap yarn onto a dpn. With RS facing, rejoin working yarn at first st, K8. Repeat all instructions above for the leg and paw.

Stuff legs carefully using a dpn from the outside to shift stuffing down into the paws.

• Body

Seam first 5 rows of the top of chest together in the back, forming a circle at the top. Sts are now picked up along the edge of your work to begin the body. Continue working with 1 strand of yarn and smaller-size dpns.

- 1st dpn: PU 15 sts from the top center seam to right leg
- 2nd dpn: PU 20 sts from outside of right leg to outside of left leg
- 3rd dpn: PU 15 sts from left leg to the top center seam (50 sts)

Rows 2–10 and 34–38 are short rows worked back and forth over just some of the sts; turn your work after each one. Knitting in the round over all the sts resumes in rounds 11 and 39, respectively.

Rnd 1: K all sts.
Row 2: K 2, w&t.
Row 3: P4, w&t.
Row 4: K6, w&t.
Row 5: P8, w&t.
Row 6: K10, w&t.
Row 7: P12, w&t.
Row 8: K14, w&t.
Row 9: P16, w&t.
Row 10: K8 (EOR).
Rnd 11: K23, SSK, K2tog, K23. (48 sts)
Rnds 12–19: K all sts.
Rnd 20: K22, SSK, K2tog, K22. (46 sts)
Rnd 21: K all sts.
Rnd 22: K21, SSK, K2tog, K21. (44 sts)
Rnd 23: K all sts.
Rnd 24: K20, SSK, K2tog, K20. (42 sts)
Rnds 25–28: K all sts.
Rnd 29: K19, SSK, K2tog, K19. (40 sts)
Rnds 30–33: K all sts.
Row 34: K6, w&t.
Row 35: P12, w&t.
Row 36: K14, w&t.
Row 37: P16, w&t.
Row 38: K8 (EOR).
Rnd 39: K18, SSK, K2tog, K18. (38 sts)
Rnds 40–43: K all sts.
Rnd 44: K17, SSK, K2tog, K17. (36 sts)
Rnds 45–52: K all sts.
Rnd 53: (Creating a hole for the tail) Cast off first 2 sts, K31, 2 sts remain on last needle. Slip the 2nd of these 2 sts over the last st and

off needle. K the last st. Pull 2nd to last st on working needle over the last st and off needle. Total of 4 sts cast off. CO 2 new sts to end of round.
Rnd 54: CO 2 new sts to working needle, K34. (36 sts)
Rnd 55: K all sts.
Rnd 56: (K2tog, K2) 9 times. (27 sts)
Rnd 57: K all sts.
Rnd 58: (K2tog, K1) 9 times. (18 sts)
Rnd 59: K all sts.
Rnd 60: (K2tog) 9 times. (9 sts)

Cut yarn, thread through remaining live sts, and pull closed. Weave in loose end.

• Tail

Continue working with smaller-size dpns and one strand of color A. Beginning at center/bottom of tail opening, PU 12 sts with 3 dpns around opening.

Rnds 1–5: K all rounds.
Rnd 6: K1, M1R, K10, M1L, K1. (14 sts)
Rnds 7–16: K all sts.
Rnd 17: K1, M1R, K12, M1L, K1. (16 sts)
Rnds 18–27: K all sts.
Rnd 28: K2tog, K12, SSK. (14 sts)
Rnds 29–30: K all sts.
Rnd 31: K2tog, K10, SSK. (12 sts)
Rnds 32–33: K all sts.
Rnd 34: K2tog, K8, SSK. (10 sts)
Rnd 35: K all sts.

Rnd 36: K2tog, K6, SSK. (8 sts)

Cut yarn, thread through remaining live sts, and pull closed. Body and tail can be stuffed at this point.

• Upper Back Leg (make 2)

The back legs are worked separately and in two pieces: upper and lower. The two pieces are then seamed together, and the combined piece is seamed to body.

Continuing with color A and size 5 dpns, CO 13 sts onto 3 dpns. Join in the round by slipping the first CO st onto the 3rd needle and then pulling the 2nd stitch (formerly the last st) over it and off the needle; 12 sts remain.

Rnd 1: K all sts.
Rnd 2: (K1, M1R, K4, M1L, K1) 2 times. (16 sts)
Rnd 3: K all sts.
Rnd 4: (K1, M1R, K6, M1L, K1) 2 times. (20 sts)
Rnd 5: K all sts.
Rnd 6: (K1, M1R, K8, M1L, K1) 2 times. (24 sts)
Rnds 7–26: K all sts.
Rnd 27: (K1, K2tog, K6, SSK, K1) 2 times. (20 sts)
Rnd 28: K all sts.
Rnd 29: (K1, K2tog, K4, SSK, K1) 2 times. (16 sts)
Rnd 30: K all sts.
Rnd 31: (K1, K2tog, K2, SSK, K1) 2 times. (12 sts)
Rnd 32: K all sts.

Cut yarn, thread through remaining live sts, and pull closed. Stuff loosely through the CO end. Piece should be flat rather than round.

Pass the CO tail underneath every other CO st; pull to cinch closed. Weave in loose ends.

• Lower Back Leg (make 2)

With color A, CO 17 sts onto three size 5 dpns. Join in the round by slipping the first CO st onto the 3rd needle and then pulling the 2nd stitch (formerly the last st) over it and off the needle; 16 sts remain. Rows 19–21 are short rows worked on just some of the sts.

Rnd 1: K all sts.
Rnd 2: SSK, K12, K2tog. (14 sts)
Rnd 3: SSK, K10, K2tog. (12 sts)
Rnd 4: SSK, K8, K2tog. (10 sts)
Rnd 5: SSK, K6, K2tog. (8 sts)
Rnds 6–13: K all sts.
Rnd 14: (M1, K1) 2 times, K4, (M1, K1) 2 times. (12 sts)
Rnds 15–18: K all sts.
Row 19: K4, w&t.

Row 20: P8, w&t.
Row 21: K4 (EOR).

Cut yarn, thread through live sts, and pull closed. Stuff through the CO edge. Seam the CO edge (with decreases pointed up) to the upper leg piece about 4 rows up from the bottom at a right angle.

The upper legs are then positioned at the end of the body, with knitted rows running at the same angle and direction as the knitted rows of the body. Upper legs should be about 3 rows from the back and bottom (cast-off section) of body.

Seam the upper leg to body from lower leg at the bottom about three-quarters of the way to the top. This allows for the top of the upper leg to fall outward.

• Neck

This section is worked flat on size 8 dpns with yarn held double, using the intarsia method of colorwork as with the chest. Work is turned at the end of each row.

You will need 2 balls of color A held double and 1 ball of color B held double just as you did for the chest. Sts are picked up in the original CO sts to work this section; begin at center/back of neck.

- 1st dpn (with color A): (PU 2, yo) 4 times in the color A CO sts (12 sts)
- 2nd dpn (with color B): PU 12 in the color B CO sts (12 sts)
- 3rd dpn (with color A): (Yo, PU 2) 4 times in the color A CO sts (12 sts)

Row 1: Color A: P12; Color B: P12; Color A: P12.
Row 2: Color A: SSK, K10 (11 sts); Color B: K4, SSK, K2tog, K4 (10 sts); Color A: K10, K2tog (11 sts).
Row 3: Color A: P11; Color B: P10; Color A: P11.
Row 4: Color A: SSK, K10; Color B: K8 (8 sts); Color A: K10, SSK.
Row 5: Color A: P11; Color B: P8; Color A: P11.
Row 6: Color A: SSK, K9 (10 sts); Color B: K2, SSK, K2tog, K2 (6 sts); Color A: K9, K2tog (10 sts).
Row 7: Color A: P10; Color B: P6; Color A: P10.
Row 8: Color A: SSK, K9 (10 sts); Color B: K4 (4 sts); Color A: K9, K2tog (10 sts).
Row 9: Color A: P10; Color B: P4; Color A: P10.
Row 10: Color A: SSK, K9 (10 sts); Color B: K2 (2 sts); Color A: K9, K2tog (10 sts).

22 sts remain. Cut the first ball of color A (RS facing) and the ball of color B.

• Head

Join sts in the round, continuing to use size 8 dpns and color A yarn held double. Rows 2–8 are short rows worked back and forth over just some of the sts; turn your work after each one. Knitting in the round over all the sts resumes in round 9.
Rnd 1: K all sts.
Row 2: K1, w&t.
Row 3: P2, w&t.
Row 4: K3, w&t.
Row 5: P4, w&t.
Row 6: K5, w&t.
Row 7: P6, w&t.
Row 8: K3 (EOR).
Rnd 9: K1, M1, K2, M1, K16, M1, K2, M1, K1. (26 sts)
Rnd 10: K all sts.
Rnd 11: K3, SSK, K2tog, K12, SSK, K2tog, K3. (22 sts)
Rnd 12: K2, SSK, K2tog, K10, SSK, K2tog, K2. (18 sts)
Rnd 13: K1, SSK, K2tog, K8, SSK, K2tog, K1. (14 sts)
Rnds 14–15: K all sts.
Rnd 16: K1, SSK, K2tog, K4, SSK, K2tog, K1. (10 sts)
Rnds 17–19: K all sts.

Switch to size 5 dpns for the remainder of the pattern, continuing to work in the round with color A held double. The upper jaw is shaped first.
Rnd 20: K3, place 4 on scrap yarn, CO 4 new sts to working dpn, K3. (10 sts)
Rnd 21: K all sts.
Rnd 22: K1, (SSK, K2tog) 2 times, K1. (6 sts)
Rnd 23: K2tog, K2, SSK. (4 sts)

Cut yarn, thread through remaining live sts, pull closed tightly. Weave in loose end.

Place 4 sts from scrap yarn onto one size 5 dpn. With WS facing, rejoin double strand of color A at 1st st. The lower jaw is worked flat; turn work after each row.
Row 1: P4.
Row 2: SSK, K2. (3 sts)
Row 3: P2tog, P1, pass 1st st over (cast off 1). (1 st)

Cut yarn and pull through last st. Weave loose end down edge of work, and thread through base of jaw to the other side. Pull edges together slightly to keep lower jaw from rolling outward.

Adjust stuffing as needed in the body, legs, and chest through hole at back of neck and then stuff neck and head; seam hole closed.

• Ears (make 2)

CO 13 sts onto three size 5 dpns with 1 strand of color A. Join in the round by slipping the first CO st onto the 3rd needle and then pulling the 2nd stitch (formerly the last st) over it and off the needle; 12 sts remain.
Rnd 1: K all sts.
Rnd 2: K2tog, K4, SSK, K4. (10 sts)
Rnd 3: K all sts.
Rnd 4: K2tog, K3, SSK, K3. (8 sts)
Rnd 5: K all sts.

Cut yarn, thread through remaining live sts, and pull closed. Weave in loose end. Flatten front to back, fold CO edge together slightly, creating a slight hollow in the center. Seam to head in a downward direction with CO tail.

• Finishing

With color C, embroider eyes as straight lines on sides of head midway between nose and ears and about 4 sts apart.

Nose is embroidered with color C.

Front legs should be positioned under chest and go straight down, as opposed to at an angle and in front of chest. A piece of yarn can be threaded from one paw to the other to maintain this position and keep them closer together. All 4 legs may need to be supported in order to stand properly.

Wide variety of habitats including wet and dry forests, shrubland, and grasslands.

Asian Elephants are highly intelligent, have strong family bonds, sophisticated forms of communication, and complex behavior

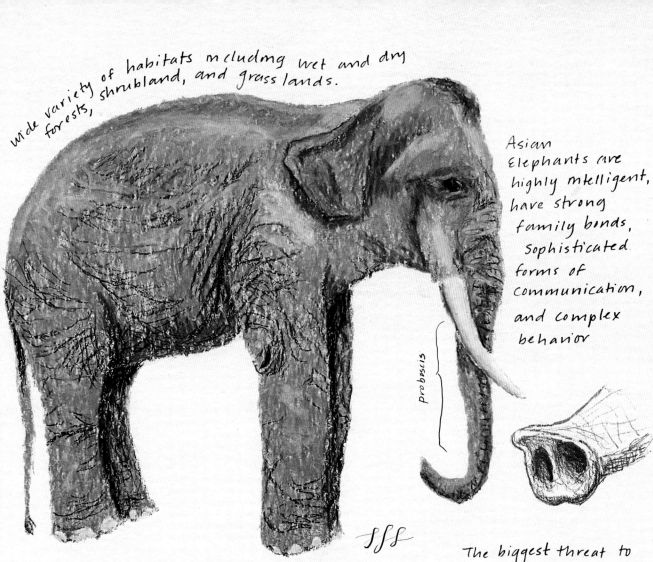

Proboscis

The biggest threat to Asian elephants is habitat loss and fragmentation.

ASIAN ELEPHANT

* Sighted at Bandipur National Park, Karnataka, India

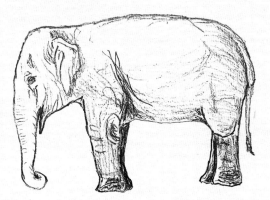

Female asian elephants rarely have tusks and only some of the males have them.

Asian Elephant

SIZE

11"/28 cm long
5"/12.5 cm wide

YARN

Cascade 220, #4 medium weight, 100%
Peruvian Highland wool, 220 yd./200 m per
3.5 oz./100 g skein
- A suggestions: 8401 Silver Grey; 2442 Fog
  Hatt; 1009 Storm Cloud (everything but tusks);
  190 yd./174 m
- B (optional): 8010 Natural; (tusks); 5 yd./4.5 m

NEEDLES

US size 3/3.25 mm dpns

NOTIONS

7 mm black safety eyes
Darning needle
Nickels for stabilizing legs (optional)
Pipe cleaner (optional)
Stuffing

INSTRUCTIONS

• Front Left Leg

This pattern begins at the bottom of the front
left foot, proceeds up the left leg, across the
back, and then down the right leg to the bottom
of the front right foot. CO 19 sts onto 3 dpns.
Join in the round by slipping the first CO st onto
the 3rd needle and then pulling the 2nd stitch
(formerly the last st) over it and off the needle; 18
sts remain.

Rnds 1–2: K all sts.
Rnd 3: (K2tog, K1) 6 times. (12 sts)
Rnds 4–8: K all sts.
Rnd 9: (M1R, K5, M1L, K1) 2 times. (16 sts)
Rnds 10–21: K all sts.
Rnd 22: (M1R, K1) 2 times, K12, (M1L, K1) 2 times.
  (20 sts)
Rnds 23–24: K all sts.
Rnd 25: M1R, K19, M1L, K1. (22 sts)
Rnds 26–34: K all sts.

I recommend that you work the sections of this
pattern in the order written and do not stuff
any part of your elephant until the proboscis
is completed. Stuffing before that will make
knitting difficult.

Rnd 35: K10, cut working yarn, place next 8 sts on
  scrap yarn, rejoin yarn at next st on needle, K4.
  (14 sts)
Rnd 36: K10, arrange all 14 sts on 1 dpn (EOR).
  The remainder of the left leg is worked flat,
turning work after each row.
Row 37: P14.
Row 38: SSK, K12. (13 sts)
Row 39: P13.
Row 40: K13.
Row 41: P13.
Row 42: SSK, K11. (12 sts)
Row 43: P12.
Row 44: K12.
Row 45: P12.
Row 46: SSK, K10. (11 sts)
Row 47: P11.
Row 48: K11. (11 sts)
Row 49: P11.
Row 50: SSK, K9. (10 sts)
Row 51: P10.
Row 52: K10.
Row 53: P10.
Row 54: SSK, K8. (9 sts)
Row 55: P9.
Row 56: K9.
Row 57: P9.
Row 58: SSK, K7. (8 sts)
Row 59: P8.
Row 60: K8.
Row 61: P8.
Row 62: SSK, K6. (7 sts)
Row 63: P7.
Row 64: K7.
Row 65: P7.

• Front Right Leg

Continue with sts from front left leg.

Row 1: K1, M1L, K6. (8 sts)
Row 2: P8.
Row 3: K8.
Row 4: P8.
Row 5: K1, M1L, K7. (9 sts)
Row 6: P9.
Row 7: K9.
Row 8: P9.
Row 9: K1, M1L, K8. (10 sts)
Row 10: P10.
Row 11: K10.
Row 12: P10.
Row 13: K1, M1L, K9. (11 sts)
Row 14: P11.
Row 15: K11.
Row 16: P11.
Row 17: K1, M1L, K10. (12 sts)
Row 18: P12.
Row 19: K12.
Row 20: P12.
Row 21: K1, M1L, K11. (13 sts)
Row 22: P13.
Row 23: K13.
Row 24: P13.
Row 25: K1, M1L, K12. (14 sts)
Row 26: P14.
Row 27: K14, arrange sts on 2 dpns, CO 8 new sts to a 3rd dpn, join sts in the round (EOR). (22 sts)
Rnds 28–36: K all sts.
Rnd 37: K2tog, K18, SSK. (20 sts)
Rnds 38–39: K all sts.
Rnd 40: (K2tog, K1) 2 times, K8, (SSK, K1) 2 times. (16 sts)
Rnds 41–52: K all sts.
Rnd 53: (K2tog, K2) 4 times. (12 sts)
Rnds 54–58: K all sts.
Rnd 59: K3, (M1L, K1) 3 times, (K1, M1R) 3 times, K3. (18 sts)
Rnds 60–61: K all sts.
Cast off all sts.

• Strip between Legs

Place 8 sts from scrap yarn onto 1 dpn. With RS facing, rejoin working yarn at first st; K8. Work a total of 6 rows back and forth in stockinette st; cast off. Seam cast-off edge to the 8 CO sts on the inside of the right leg.

• Body

Sts are now picked up around the edge of the back side of the work to begin the body. The back side is identified by the "elbows" that protrude where the increased sts are on the legs.

With RS facing and working on the back side, begin at the top/center and pick up the following sts with 3 dpns:

- 1st dpn: PU 22 sts along the edge from top/center down to the right leg
- 2nd dpn: PU 10 sts along the edge of the center strip from right leg to left leg
- 3rd dpn: PU 22 sts along the edge from the center strip to the top/center (EOR)
  Join 54 sts in the round.

Rnd 1: K21, (Kfb) 12 times, K21. (66 sts)
Rnds 2–9: K all sts.
Rnd 10: K1, M1R, K64, M1L, K1. (68 sts)
Rnds 11–13: K all sts.
Rnd 14: K1, M1R, K66, M1L, K1. (70 sts)
Rnds 15–17: K all sts.
Rnd 18: K1, M1R, K68, M1L, K1. (72 sts)
Rnds 19–26: K all sts.
Rnd 27: K1, K2tog, K66, SSK, K1. (70 sts)
Rnds 28–29: K all sts.
Rnd 30: K1, K2tog, K64, SSK, K1. (68 sts)
Rnds 31–32: K all sts.
Rnd 33: K1, K2tog, K62, SSK, K1. (66 sts)
Rnd 34: K all sts.

Short rows are now worked back and forth over just some of the sts on both sides of the EOR. These will shape the rear end of your elephant.

Row 35: K6, w&t.
Row 36: P12, w&t.

Row 37: K13, w&t.
Row 38: P14, w&t.
Row 39: K15, w&t.
Row 40: P16, w&t.
Row 41: K17, w&t.
Row 42: P18, w&t.
Row 43: K19, w&t.
Row 44: P20, w&t.
Row 45: K21, w&t.
Row 46: P22, w&t.
Row 47: K23, w&t.
Row 48: P24, w&t.
Row 49: K25, w&t.
Row 50: P26, w&t.
Row 51: K27, w&t.
Row 52: P28, w&t.
Row 53: K29, w&t.
Row 54: P30, w&t.
Row 55: K31, w&t.
Row 56: P32, w&t.
Row 57: K15 (1 st short of the EOR).

Place the last st of the round together with the first st of the next round on a piece of scrap yarn. These 2 sts are used for working the tail after the back legs are finished. Pull working yarn across the small hole created for the tail; short rows are resumed.

Row 58: K16, w&t.
Row 59: P32, w&t.
Row 60: K33, w&t.
Row 61: P34, w&t.
Row 62: K35, w&t.
Row 63: P36, w&t.
Row 64: K18 (EOR).
Row 65: K32, place remaining 32 on scrap yarn.

• Back Right Leg

Arrange the first 32 sts onto 3 dpns and join in the round. This leg will extend backward slightly.
Rnds 1–3: K all sts. (32 sts)
Rnd 4: (K6, SSK, K2tog, K6) 2 times. (28 sts)
Rnds 5–6: K all sts.
Rnd 7: (K5, SSK, K2tog, K5) 2 times. (24 sts)
Rnds 8–9: K all sts.
Rnd 10: (K4, SSK, K2tog, K4) 2 times. (20 sts)
Rnds 11–12: K all sts.
Rnd 13: (K3, SSK, K2tog, K3) 2 times. (16 sts)
Rnds 14–24: K all sts.
Rnd 25: (K2tog, K2) 4 times. (12 sts)
Rnds 26–30: K all sts.

Rnd 31: K5, (M1L, K1) 3 times, (K1, M1R) 3 times, K1. (18 sts)
Rnds 32–33: K all sts.
Cast off.

• Back Left Leg

Place 32 sts from scrap yarn onto 3 dpns. With WS facing, rejoin working yarn at first st on top (formerly the last st of the round). Short rows are added to the beginning of this leg to change the direction of the work and point the leg straight downward. Turn work without wrapping on the even rows.
Row 1: P8, w&t.
Row 2: K8.
Row 3: P10, w&t.
Row 4: K10.
Row 5: P12, w&t.
Row 6: K12.
Row 7: P14, w&t.
Row 8: K14.
Join sts in the round.
Rnd 9: (K6, SSK, K2tog, K6) 2 times. (28 sts)
Rnds 10–11: K all sts.
Rnd 12: (K5, SSK, K2tog, K5) 2 times. (24 sts)
Rnds 13–14: K all sts.
Rnd 15: (K4, SSK, K2tog, K4) 2 times. (20 sts)
Rnds 16–17: K all sts.
Rnd 18: (K3 SSK, K2tog, K3) 2 times. (16 sts)
Rnds 19–29: K all sts.
Rnd 30: (K2tog, K2) 4 times. (12 sts)
Rnds 31–35: K all sts.
Rnd 36: (M1L, K1) 2 times, (K1, M1R) 3 times, K6, M1L, K1. (18 sts)
Rnds 37–38: K all sts.
Cast off.

• Tail

Place the 2 sts from scrap yarn onto 1 dpn. Sts are now picked up around the small hole beneath the 2 sts to begin the tail. Begin at the bottom/center of the hole and pick up/work the following sts with 3 dpns:

- 1st dpn: With RS facing, PU 3 sts along the left side of the hole
- 2nd dpn: K the 2 sts on the dpn
- 3rd dpn: PU 3 sts along the right side of the hole (8 sts); EOR
  Join the round.

Rnds 1–3: K all sts.
Rnd 4: K2tog, K4, SSK. (6 sts)
Rnds 5–8: K all sts.
Rnd 9: K2tog, K2, SSK all on 1 dpn. (4 sts)
Rnds 10–14: Work 5 rows of a 4-st I-cord.
Rnd 15: K2tog, K2. (3 sts)
Rnds 16–20: Work 5 rows of a 3-st I-cord.
Rnd 21: K2tog, K1. (2 sts)
Rnds 22–26: Work 5 rows of a 2-st I-cord.

Cut yarn, thread through 2 sts, and pull closed. Weave in loose ends. Add a few pieces of yarn to the end; trim evenly. Separate the plies to make it slightly fluffy. Leave the hole between the back legs open for now.

• Beginning of Head

Begin by cutting a piece of working yarn about 1 yard in length; set aside for bottom lip.

Sts are now picked up around the edge of the front side of the opening (opposite of where sts for the body were picked up) to begin the head. With RS facing, begin at top/center of opening and PU the following sts with 3 dpns:

- 1st dpn: PU 20 sts along the edge from top/center down to the left leg
- 2nd dpn: PU 6 sts along the edge of the center strip from the left leg to the right one
- 3rd dpn: PU 20 sts along the edge from the center strip to the top/center (EOR)
  46 sts total; join in the round. Sts can be rearranged on the needles after picking them up.

Rnd 1: K all sts.
Rnd 2: (K2tog, K3) 4 times, K6, (K2tog, K3) 4 times. (38 sts)
Rnds 3–4: K all sts.
Rnd 5: (M1, K2) 8 times, K6, (M1, K2) 8 times. (54 sts)
Rnds 6–12: K all sts.

Rows 13–24 are short rows that will create 2 bumps on the top of your elephant's head, a characteristic of the Asian elephant. Each of the bumps is worked separately.

1st bump; working on the left side of the EOR (beginning of round).
Row 13: K1, M1R, K3, w&t. (55 sts)
Row 14: P4, w&t.
Row 15: K5, w&t.
Row 16: P5, w&t.
Row 17: K6, w&t.
Row 18: P7 (EOR).

2nd bump; working on the right side of the EOR (end of round).
Row 19: P1, M1P, P3, w&t. (56 sts)
Row 20: K4, w&t.
Row 21: P5, w&t.
Row 22: K5, w&t.
Row 23: P6, w&t.
Row 24: K7 (EOR).

• Bottom Lip

The majority of the sts are now placed on scrap yarn so that the bottom lip can be worked separately.

Setup: Place the first 23 sts on a piece of scrap yarn, leave the center 10 sts on a dpn, and place the last 23 sts on a piece of scrap yarn. Use the 1-yard length of yarn that was set aside for rounds 1–4.
With RS facing, join yarn at first st, K10. Arrange these 10 sts onto 3 dpns and join in the round.

Rnd 1: K all sts.
Rnd 2: K3, SSK, K2tog, K3. (8 sts)
Rnd 3: K all sts.
Rnd 4: K2, SSK, K2tog, K2. (6 sts)

Cut yarn, thread through remaining live sts, and pull closed. Weave in loose ends.

• Head Continued

Setup: Place the first 23 sts back onto a dpn, K23. CO 10 new sts to a 2nd dpn, place the last 23 sts back onto a 3rd dpn, K23. (56 sts)
Rows 2–16 are short rows that are worked back and forth over just some of the sts on both sides of the EOR. These will change the direction of the knitting and shape the beginning of the proboscis.

Rnd 1: K all sts.
Row 2: K8, SSK, K2tog, w&t. (54 sts)
Row 3: P22, w&t.

Row 4: SSK, K2tog, K15, SSK, K2tog, w&t. (50 sts)
Row 5: P20, w&t.
Row 6: SSK, K2tog, K13, SSK, K2tog, w&t. (46 sts)
Row 7: P18, w&t.
Row 8: SSK, K2tog, K11, SSK, K2tog, w&t. (42 sts)
Row 9: P16, w&t.
Row 10: SSK, K2tog, K9, SSK, K2tog, w&t. (38 sts)
Row 11: P14, w&t.
Row 12: SSK, K2tog, K7, SSK, K2tog, w&t. (34 sts)
Row 13: P12, w&t.
Row 14: SSK, K2tog, K5, SSK, K2tog, w&t. (30 sts)
Row 15: P10, w&t.
Row 16: SSK, K2tog, K2 (EOR). (28 sts)

Attach safety eyes about 13 rows down from the short row bumps on head and about 8 sts apart from each other on top.

• Proboscis

Continue working in the round from the sts above.
Rnd 1: K11, SSK, K2, K2tog, K11. (26 sts)
Rnd 2: K all sts.
Rnd 3: K10, SSK, K2, K2tog, K10. (24 sts)
Rnd 4: K all sts.
Rnd 5: K10, SSK, K2tog, K10. (22 sts)
Rnds 6-7: K all sts.
Rnd 8: K9, SSK, K2tog, K9. (20 sts)
Rnds 9-10: K all sts.
Rnd 11: K8, SSK, K2tog, K8. (18 sts)
Rnds 12-14: K all sts.
Rnd 15: K7, SSK, K2tog, K7. (16 sts)
Rnds 16-18: K all sts.
Rnd 19: K6, SSK, K2tog, K6. (14 sts)
Rnds 20-23: K all sts.
Rnd 24: K5, SSK, K2tog, K5. (12 sts)
Rnds 25-28: K all sts.
Rnd 29: K4, SSK, K2tog, K4. (10 sts)
Rnds 30-34: K all rounds.
Rnd 35: K3, SSK, K2tog, K3. (8 sts)
Rnds 36-40: K all sts.
Rnd 41: K2, SSK, K2tog, K2. (6 sts)
Rnds 42-46: K all sts.
Rnd 47: (M1, K2) 3 times. (9 sts)
Rnd 48: K all sts.
Rnd 49: K1, w&t.
Rnd 50: P2, w&t.
Rnd 51: K1 (EOR).

Cast off, and weave in loose ends.

Stuff your elephant now, using a dpn from the outside to help shift the stuffing around and spread it evenly throughout. Legs can be stuffed through the bottom of each one; back half of body can be stuffed through hole between legs; front half of body, head, and proboscis can be stuffed through the mouth opening. Stuff fully and firmly, rounding out the rear end, stiffening the legs, and emphasizing the bumps on top of the head. The body and legs take more stuffing than you would think. The proboscis should be stuffed loosely to facilitate bending. A pipe stem cleaner can be added if desired.

To make it look like your elephant is walking, encourage the back right leg to extend backward and the back left leg to go straight down. For the same effect, the front right leg can be seamed to the body from the elbow upward. This will direct it backward to be at the same angle as the back right leg. Nickels can be added on the bottom of the feet after stuffing the legs and before sewing on the bottom of the feet, to make the elephant more stable and able to stand on its own.

After stuffing, seam the hole between the legs closed from side to side. The lower edge of the proboscis (upper lip) can be seamed to the inner edge of the bottom lip, if desired. If adding tusks, seam those inside the lower lip before seaming the mouth shut.

• Left Ear

The ears are worked separately and seamed to the head. CO 4 sts onto 1 dpn and work the following rows back and forth.

Row 1: P4.
Row 2: K1, M1L, K3. (5 sts)
Row 3: P5.
Row 4: K1, M1L, K4. (6 sts)
Row 5: P6.
Row 6: K1, M1L, K5. (7 sts)
Row 7: P7.
Row 8: K1, M1L, K6. (8 sts)
Row 9: P8.
Row 10: K1, M1L, K7. (9 sts)
Row 11: P9.
Row 12: K1, M1L, K8. (10 sts)
Row 13: P10.
Row 14: K1, M1L, K9. (11 sts)
Row 15: P11.
Row 16: K11.
Row 17: P11.
Row 18: SSK, K9. (10 sts)
Row 19: P10.
Row 20: SSK, K8. (9 sts)
Row 21: P9.
Row 22: SSK, K7. (8 sts)
Row 23: P8.
Row 24: (SSK) 4 times. (4 sts)

Cast off. Roll top edge down a little, using loose end to seam the roll in place. With RS facing forward, seam left (straight) side of ear to the left side of the head.

• Right Ear

CO 4 sts to 1 dpn.
Row 1: P4.
Row 2: K3, M1R, K1. (5 sts)
Row 3: P5.
Row 4: K4, M1R, K1. (6 sts)
Row 5: P6.
Row 6: K5, M1R, K1. (7 sts)
Row 7: P7.
Row 8: K6, M1R, K1. (8 sts)
Row 9: P8.
Row 10: K7, M1R, K1. (9 sts)
Row 11: P9.
Row 12: K8, M1R, K1. (10 sts)
Row 13: P10.
Row 14: K9, M1R, K1. (11 sts)
Row 15: P11.
Row 16: K11.

Row 17: P11.
Row 18: K9, K2tog. (10 sts)
Row 19: P10.
Row 20: K8, K2tog. (9 sts)
Row 21: P9.
Row 22: K7, K2tog. (8 sts)
Row 23: P8.
Row 24: (K2tog) 4 times. (4 sts)

Cast off. Roll top edge down a little toward the RS, using loose end to seam the roll in place. With RS facing forward, seam right (straight) side of ear to the right side of the head. The ears can bend backward or stick out to the sides in any manner, all of which are normal for Asian elephant ears.

• Tusks

Tusks are optional. Only some Asian elephant males have them; no females do.

With color B, CO 6 sts onto 1 dpn.
Rows 1–3: Work 3 rows of a 6-st I-cord.
Row 4: K2tog, K4. (5 sts)
Rows 5–7: Work 3 rows of a 5-st I-cord.
Row 8: K2tog, K3. (4 sts)
Rows 9–11: Work 3 rows of a 4-st I-cord.
Row 12: K2tog, K2. (3 sts)
Rows 13–15: Work 3 rows of a 3-st I-cord.
Row 16: K2tog, K1. (2 sts)

Cut yarn, thread through remaining live sts, and pull closed. Weave in loose ends. Seam tusks beneath the upper lip on each side with color A.

• Bottom of Feet (make 4 the same)

CO 6 sts onto 1 dpn. The bottoms of the feet are worked flat.
Row 1: P6.
Row 2: K6.
Row 3: P6.
Row 4: K1, M1L, K4, M1R, K1. (8 sts)
Row 5: P8.
Row 6: SSK, K4, K2tog. (6 sts)
Row 7: P6.

Cast off. Seam to the bottom of each foot with color A.

• Finishing

Embroidery with color A can be added above and/or below the eyes to make them look deeper set, if desired.

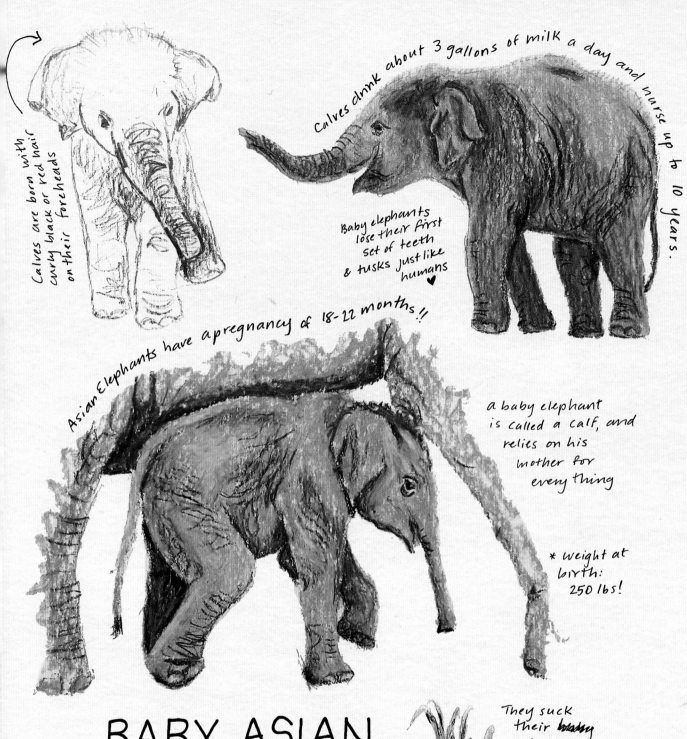

Calves are born with curly black or red hair on their foreheads

Calves drink about 3 gallons of milk a day and nurse up to 10 years.

Baby elephants lose their first set of teeth & tusks just like humans ♥

Asian Elephants have a pregnancy of 18-22 months !!

a baby elephant is called a calf, and relies on his mother for every thing

* weight at birth: 250 lbs!

BABY ASIAN ELEPHANT

✷ Sighted at Bandipur National Park, Karnataka, India

They suck their ~~baby~~ trunk as a human baby might suck its thumb "

Baby Asian Elephant

SIZE

7"/18 cm long
3"/7.5 cm wide

YARN

Cascade 220, #4 medium weight, 100%
Peruvian Highland wool, 220 yd./200 m per
3.5 oz./100 g skein
- A suggestions: 8401 Silver Grey; 2442 Fog Hatt;
  1009 Storm Cloud; 30 yd./27.5 m

NEEDLES

US size 3/3.25 mm dpns

NOTIONS

5 mm black safety eyes
Darning needle
Stitch markers
Stuffing

INSTRUCTIONS

• Front Left Leg

This pattern begins at the bottom of the front
left foot, proceeds up the left leg, across the
back, and then down the right leg to the bottom
of the front right foot. CO 13 sts onto 3 dpns.
Join in the round by slipping the first CO st onto
the 3rd needle and then pulling the 2nd stitch
(formerly the last st) over it and off the needle;
12 sts remain. It is helpful to identify the EOR by
placing a st marker.
Rnds 1–2: K all sts.
Rnd 3: K2tog, K8, SSK. (10 sts)
Rnds 4–13: K all sts.
Rnd 14: (M1R, K1) 2 times, K6, (M1L, K1) 2 times.
   (14 sts)
Rnds 15–20: K all sts.
Rnd 21: K6, cut working yarn, place next 4 sts on
   scrap yarn, rejoin yarn at next st on needle, K4.
   (10 sts)
Rnd 22: K6, arrange all 10 sts on 1 dpn (EOR).
Rnd 23: P10.
Rnd 24: SSK, K8. (9 sts)
Rnd 25: P9.
Rnd 26: SSK, K7. (8 sts)

Rnd 27: P8.
Rnd 28 : SSK, K6. (7 sts)
Rnd 29: P7.
Rnd 30: SSK, K5. (6 sts)
Rnd 31: P6.
Rnd 32: SSK, K4. (5 sts)
Rnd 33: P5.
Rnd 34: SSK, K3. (4 sts)
Rnds 35–41: Work 7 rows straight stockinette
   stitch.

• Front Right Leg

Rnds 1–8: Work 8 rows straight stockinette st.
Rnd 9: K1, M1L, K3. (5 sts)
Rnd 10: P5.
Rnd 11: K1, M1L, K4. (6 sts)
Rnd 12: P6.
Rnd 13: K1, M1L, K5. (7 sts)
Rnd 14: P7.
Rnd 15: K1, M1L, K6. (8 sts)
Rnd 16: P8.
Rnd 17: K1, M1L, K7. (9 sts)
Rnd 18: P9.
Rnd 19: K1, M1L, K8. (10 sts)
Rnd 20: P10.
Rnd 21: K10, arrange sts on 2 dpns, CO 4 new sts
   to a 3rd dpn, join in the round. (14 sts)
Rnds 22–27: K all sts.
Rnd 28: (K2tog, K1) 2 times, K2, (SSK, K1) 2 times.
   (10 sts)
Rnds 29–38: K all sts.
Rnd 39: M1R, K9, M1L, K1. (12 sts)
Rnds 40–41: K all sts.
   Cast off. Weave in loose ends.

• Strip between Legs

Place 4 sts from scrap yarn onto 1 dpn. With RS
facing, rejoin working yarn at first st, K4. Work a
total of 4 rows back and forth in stockinette st;
cast off. Seam cast-off edge to the 4 CO sts on
the inside of the right leg.

• Body

Sts are now picked up around the edge of the
back side of the work to begin the body. The back
side is identified by the "elbows" that protrude
where the increased sts are on the legs.

With RS facing, begin at the top/center and pick up the following sts with 3 dpns:

- 1st dpn: PU 14 sts along the edge from top/center down to the right leg
- 2nd dpn: PU 6 sts along the edge of the center strip from the right leg to the left one
- 3rd dpn: PU 14 sts along the edge from the center strip to the top/center (EOR)
  Join 34 sts in the round.

Rnd 1: K14, (Kfb) 6 times, K14. (40 sts)
Rnd 2: K all sts.
Rnd 3: M1R, K39, M1L, K1. (42 sts)
Rnds 4–5: K all sts.
Rnd 6: M1R, K41, M1L, K1. (44 sts)
Rnds 7–14: K all sts.

Short rows are now worked back and forth over just some of the sts on both sides of the EOR. These will shape the rear end of your baby elephant.

Row 15: K5, w&t.
Row 16: P10, w&t.
Row 17: K11, w&t.
Row 18: P12, w&t.
Row 19: K13, w&t.
Row 20: P14, w&t.
Row 21: K15, w&t.
Row 22: P16, w&t.
Row 23: K17, w&t.
Row 24: P18, w&t.
Row 25: K19, w&t.
Row 26: P20, w&t.
Row 27: K21, w&t.
Row 28: P22, w&t.
Row 29: K23, w&t.
Row 30: P24, w&t.
Row 31: K25, w&t.
Row 32: P26, w&t.
Row 33: K27, w&t.
Row 34: P28, w&t.
Row 35: K29, w&t.
Row 36: P30, w&t.
Row 37: K31, w&t.
Row 38: P32, w&t.
Row 39: K16 (EOR).

• Back Right Leg

Setup: K22, place 22 on scrap yarn. Join the first 22 sts in the round.

Rnd 1: K all sts.

Rnd 2: K3, SSK, K2tog, K8, SSK, K2tog, K3. (18 sts)

Rnd 3: K all sts.

Rnd 4: K2, SSK, K2tog, K6, SSK, K2tog, K2. (14 sts)

Rnd 5: K all sts.

Rnd 6: K1, SSK, K2tog, K4, SSK, K2tog, K1. (10 sts)

Rnds 7-14: K all sts.

Rnd 15: M1R, K9, M1L, K1. (12 sts)

Rnds 16-17: K all sts.

Cast off.

• Back Left Leg

Setup: Place 22 sts from scrap yarn onto 3 dpns. Rejoin yarn at next st on needle (bottom of your baby elephant), K22. Join sts in the round and work rounds 1-17 the same as the right leg.

Stuff your baby elephant now. Since it's small, it is still easy to knit the head and proboscis if the body and legs are already stuffed. After stuffing, seam the hole between the legs closed from side to side.

• Tail

Setup: Count 9 rows up from the top of the hole between the legs. PU 2 sts in the center of that row; with same dpn, PU 2 more sts directly under the first 2. (4 sts)

Row 1: Work 1 row of a 4-st I-cord.

Row 2: K2tog, K2. (3 sts)

Row 3: Work 1 row of a 3-st I-cord.

Row 4: K2tog, K1. (2 sts)

Rows 5-16: Work 12 rows of a 2-st I-cord.

Cut yarn, thread through last 2 sts, and pull closed. Add a few pieces of yarn to the end; trim evenly. Separate the plies of yarn to make it slightly fluffy.

• Beginning of Head

Begin by cutting a piece of working yarn about 2 feet in length; set aside for bottom lip.

Sts are now picked up around the edge of the front side of the opening (opposite of where sts for the body were picked up) to begin the head. With RS facing, begin at top/center of opening and PU the following sts with 3 dpns:

- 1st dpn: PU 14 sts along the edge from top/center down to the left leg

- 2nd dpn: PU 6 sts along the edge of the center strip from the left leg to the right one

- 3rd dpn: PU 14 sts along the edge from the center strip to the top/center (EOR)

34 sts total; join in the round. Sts can be rearranged on needles after picking them up.

Rnds 1-5: K all sts.

• Bottom Lip

The majority of the sts are now placed on scrap yarn so that the bottom lip can be worked separately.

Setup: Place the first 15 sts on a piece of scrap yarn, leave the center 4 sts on a dpn, and place the last 15 sts on a piece of scrap yarn. Use the 2-foot length of yarn that was set aside for the following rounds.

With RS facing, join yarn at first st.

Rnd 1: K4.

Rnd 2: P4.

Rnd 3: SSK, K2tog. (2 sts)

Cut yarn, thread through last 2 sts, and pull closed. Weave in loose ends.

• Head Continued

Setup: Place the first 15 sts back onto a dpn, K15. CO 4 new sts to a 2nd dpn, place the last 15 sts back onto a 3rd dpn, K15. (34 sts)

Rows 3-13 are short rows that are worked back and forth over just some of the sts on both sides of the EOR. These will change the direction of the knitting and shape the beginning of the proboscis.

Rnds 1-2: K all sts.

Row 3: K5, SSK, K2tog, w&t. (32 sts)

Row 4: P16, w&t.

Row 5: SSK, K2tog, K9, SSK, K2tog, w&t. (28 sts)

Row 6: P14, w&t.

Row 7: SSK, K2tog, K7, SSK, K2tog, w&t. (24 sts)

Row 8: P12, w&t.

Row 9: SSK, K2tog, K5, SSK, K2tog, w&t. (20 sts)

Row 10: P10, w&t.

Row 11: SSK, K2tog, K3, SSK, K2tog, w&t. (16 sts)

Row 12: P8, w&t.

Row 13: SSK, K2tog, K1 (EOR). (14 sts)

• Proboscis

Continue working in the round from the sts above.

Rnd 1: K all sts.
Rnd 2: K4, SSK, K2, K2tog, K4. (12 sts)
Rnds 3–8: K all sts.
Rnd 9: K4, SSK, K2tog, K4. (10 sts)
Rnds 10–15: K all sts.
Rnd 16: K3, SSK, K2tog, K3. (8 sts)
Rnds 17–22: K all sts.
Rnd 23: K2, SSK, K2tog, K2. (6 sts)
Rnds 24–27: K all sts.
  Cast off.

  Add safety eyes through the mouth opening about 12 rows from the neckline and about 5 sts apart from each other on top. Stuff neck, head, and proboscis now. The body is stuffed fully and firmly, but the proboscis is stuffed loosely. If the bottom lip hangs down more than you would like, the mouth opening can be made narrower by stitching the sides of it closed. Likewise, the lower edge of the proboscis (upper lip) can be seamed to the inner edge of the bottom lip, if desired. Add more stuffing to the legs or body now if needed, through the mouth or from the bottom of the legs.

• Left Ear

The ears are worked separately and seamed to the head. CO 4 sts onto 1 dpn and work the rows flat.

Row 1: P4.
Row 2: K1, M1L, K3. (5 sts)
Row 3: P5.
Row 4: K1, M1L, K4. (6 sts)
Row 5: P6.
Row 6: K1, M1L, K5. (7 sts)
Row 7: P7.
Row 8: K1, M1L, K6. (8 sts)
Row 9: P8.
Row 10: SSK, K6. (7 sts)
Row 11: P7.
Row 12: SSK, K5. (6 sts)
Row 13: P6.
Row 14: (SSK) 3 times. (3 sts)
  Cast off. Roll top edge down a little, using loose end to seam the roll in place. With RS facing forward, seam left (straight) side of ear to the left side of the head.

• Right Ear

CO 4 sts to 1 dpn.

Row 1: P4.
Row 2: K3, M1R, K1. (5 sts)
Row 3: P5.
Row 4: K4, M1R, K1. (6 sts)
Row 5: P6.
Row 6: K5, M1R, K1. (7 sts)
Row 7: P7.
Row 8: K6, M1R, K1. (8 sts)
Row 9: P8.
Row 10: K6, K2tog. (7 sts)
Row 11: P7.
Row 12: K5, K2tog. (6 sts)
Row 13: P6.
Row 14: (K2tog) 3 times. (3 sts)
  Cast off. Roll top edge down a little toward the RS, using loose end to seam the roll in place. With RS facing forward, seam right (straight) side of ear to the right side of the head.

• Bottom of Feet

Stuffing in the legs is prevented from coming out by closing the bottom of the feet with a few sewn stitches going across in several directions. Use a darning needle and main color yarn for this.

The wood pigeon is the largest and most common species of the pigeon family in the UK

The wood pigeon can be differentiated from other pigeons by the large, white patches on the sides of the neck, below a smudge of iridescent green.

Grey overall, with a pinkish breast, black outer wings and a broad black band at the end of the tail.

WOOD PIGEON

* Sighted at Cartmel priory Church Yard Cartmel, Cumbria, England

a distinctive, cooing song with five distinct notes heard throughout the spring.

Wood pigeons are able to take in great amounts of food in one sitting because they store it in a crop, which is a muscular pouch in the upper chest.

Wood Pigeon

SIZE

11"/28 cm long
4.5"/11.5 cm wide

YARN

Cascade 220, #4 medium weight, 100%
Peruvian Highland wool, 220 yd./200 m per
3.5 oz./100 g skein
- A: 8509 Grey (body, head); 60 yd./55 m
- B: 1039 Helleborous Heather; 20 yd./18 m
- C: 9473 Gris (wingtips; embroidery on neck);
  10 yd./9 m
- D: 8505 White (spots on neck); 5 yd./4.5 m
- E: 8311 Mineral Blue (embroidery on neck);
  1 yd./1 m
- F: 9491 Greystone Heather (wings);
  40 yd./36.5 m
- G: 7804 Shrimp (feet and toes); 10 yd./9 m

NEEDLES

US size 3/3.25 mm dpns
US size 3/3.25 mm straight needles (optional)

NOTIONS

6 mm round safety eyes (pale yellow)
Darning needle
Scrap of any black yarn for claws
Stuffing

INSTRUCTIONS

• Breast and Body

Work begins at neckline. The breast can be
worked on either dpns or straight needles. It
is worked flat and uses the intarsia method of
colorwork. Begin by preparing a second small ball
of color A (about 10 yards) so you'll have one for
each side. CO the following number and colors of
sts onto 1 needle, starting with the smaller ball of
color A:
Color A: CO 6 sts
Color B: CO 12 sts
Color A: CO 6 sts
Row 1: Color A: P6; Color B: P12; Color A: P6.
Row 2: Color A: K6; Color B: K12; Color A: K6.
Row 3: Color A: P6; Color B: P12; Color A: P6.

Row 4: Color A: K6; Color B: K12; Color A: K6.
Row 5: Color A: P6; Color B: P12; Color A: P6.
Row 6: Color A: K5, M1L, K1 (7 sts); Color B: K1, M1R,
K10, M1L, w&t (14 sts).
Row 7: Color B: P12, w&t.
Row 8: Color B: K13; Color A: K1, M1R, K5 (7 sts).
Row 9: Color A: P7; Color B: P14; Color A: P7.
Row 10: Color A: K6, M1L, K1 (8 sts); Color B: K1,
M1R, K12, M1L, w&t (16 sts).
Row 11: Color B: P14, w&t.
Row 12: Color B: K15; Color A: K1, M1R, K6 (8 sts).
Row 13: Color A: P8; Color B: P16; Color A: P8.
Row 14: Color A: K7, M1L, K1 (9 sts); Color B: K1,
M1R, K14, M1L, w&t (18 sts).
Row 15: Color B: P16, w&t.
Row 16: Color B: K17; Color A: K1, M1R, K7 (9 sts).
Row 17: Color A: P9; Color B: P18; Color A: P9.
Row 18: Color A: K8, M1L, K1 (10 sts); Color B: K1,
M1R, K16, M1L, w&t (20 sts).
Row 19: Color B: P18, w&t.
Row 20: Color B: K19; Color A: K1, M1R, K8 (10 sts).
Row 21: Color A: P10; Color B: P20; Color A: P10.
Row 22: Color A: K9, M1L, K1 (11 sts); Color B: K1,
M1R, K18, M1L, w&t (22 sts).
Row 23: Color B: P20, w&t.
Row 24: Color B: K21; Color A: K1, M1R, K9 (11 sts).
Row 25: Color A: P11; Color B: P22; Color A: P11.
Row 26: Color A: K10, M1L, K1 (12 sts); Color B: K1,
M1R, K20, M1L, w&t (24 sts).
Row 27: Color B: P22, w&t.
Row 28: Color B: K23; Color A: K1, M1R, K10 (12 sts).
Row 29: Color A: P12; Color B: P24; Color A: P12.
Row 30: Color A: K12; Colors A and B tog: K1, M1R,
K22, M1L, w&t (26 sts).
Row 31: Colors A and B tog: P24, w&t.
Row 32: Colors A and B tog: K25; Color A: K12.
Row 33: Color A: P12; Colors A and B tog: P26;
Color A: P12.
Row 34: Color A: K12; Colors A and B tog: K1, M1R,
K24, M1, w&t (28 sts).
Row 35: Colors A and B tog: P26, w&t.
Row 36: Colors A and B tog: K27; Color A: K12.
Row 37: Color A: P12; Colors A and B tog: P28;
Color A: P12.
Row 38: Color A: K12; Colors A and B tog: K28;
Color A: K12.

Cut the first strand of color A and the strand of color B. Arrange all sts on 3 dpns, join in the round and continue knitting with the second (larger) ball of color A only.

Rows 39–50: K all sts for 12 rounds. (52 sts)

• Tail

Rnd 1: K20, (SSK, K1) 2 times, (K1, K2tog) 2 times, K20. (48 sts)

Rnds 2–3: K all sts.

Rnd 4: K18, (SSK, K1) 2 times, (K1, K2tog) 2 times, K18. (44 sts)

Rnds 5–6: K all sts.

Rnd 7: K16, (SSK, K1) 2 times, (K1, K2tog) 2 times, K16. (40 sts)

Rnds 8–9: K all sts.

Rnd 10: K14, (SSK, K1) 2 times, (K1, K2tog) 2 times, K14. (36 sts)

Rnds 11–12: K all sts.

Rnd 13: K12, (SSK, K1) 2 times, (K1, K2tog) 2 times, K12. (32 sts)

Rnds 14–15: K all sts.

Rnd 16: K10, (SSK, K1) 2 times, (K1, K2tog) 2 times, K10. (28 sts)

Rnds 17–20: K all sts.

Rnd 21: K8, (SSK, K1) 2 times, (K1, K2tog) 2 times, K8. (24 sts)

Rnds 22–25: K all sts.

Rnd 26: K6, (SSK, K1) 2 times, (K1, K2tog) 2 times, K6. (20 sts)

Rnds 27–28: K all sts.

Rnd 29: K4, (SSK, K1) 2 times, (K1, K2tog) 2 times, K4. (16 sts)

Rnds 30–31: K all sts.
Cut color A; join color C.

Rnd 32: K2, (SSK, K1) 2 times, (K1, K2tog) 2 times, K2. (12 sts)

Rnds 33–34: K all sts.

Rnd 35: K4, SSK, K2tog, K4. (10 sts)

Rnds 36–37: K all sts.

Rnd 38: K3, SSK, K2tog, K3. (8 sts)

Rnds 39–40: K all sts.
Cut yarn, thread through remaining live sts, and pull closed.

The opening of the neck and body is now closed. Join the two sides of the neck together and, with color A, seam the opening closed from the neckline down to the point where the body is worked in the round.

Stuff body now. Use a dpn from the outside to shift stuffing around and make it even, rounding out the breast. Do not stuff tail after round 16; beyond that, the tail should be left unstuffed and flattened top to bottom.

• Head

Sts are now picked up in the original CO sts to knit the head. With color A, begin in the center/back and PU 24 sts with 3 dpns. Check to make sure that sts 9–16 are centered with the front of the breast. Sts are joined in the round. Short rows are interspersed with regular rounds.

Rnd 1: K all sts.
Rnd 2: K2tog, K20, SSK. (22 sts)
Rnds 3–4: K all sts.
Rnd 5: K2tog, K18, SSK. (20 sts)
Rnd 6: K all sts.
Rnd 7: K8, SSK, K2tog, K8. (18 sts)
Row 8: K2, w&t.
Row 9: P4, w&t.
Row 10: K2 (EOR).
Rnd 11: K all sts.
Row 12: K3, w&t.
Row 13: P6, w&t.
Row 14: K3 (EOR).
Rnd 15: K all sts.
Row 16: K4, w&t.
Row 17: P8, w&t.
Row 18: K4 (EOR).
Rnd 19: K all sts.
Row 20: K5, w&t.
Row 21: P10, w&t.
Row 22: K5 (EOR).
Rnd 23: K all sts.
Row 24: K6, w&t.
Row 25: P12, w&t.
Row 26: K6 (EOR).
Rnd 27: K all sts.
Row 28: K7, w&t.
Row 29: P14, w&t.
Row 30: K7 (EOR).
Rnd 31: K all sts.
Rnd 32: K all sts.
Rnd 33: (K2tog) 3 times, K6, (SSK) 3 times. (12 sts)
Rnd 34: (K2tog) 3 times, (SSK) 3 times. (6 sts)

Safety eyes are attached now, about 5 sts apart on the top and 4 sts up from the last short row. Eyes can be embroidered if preferred after project is completed. Stuff neck and head now, adding more stuffing to body if needed. The last 4 rounds can be worked with color A or color G as desired.

Rnds 35–36: K all sts.
Rnd 37: K2tog, K2, SSK. (4 sts)
Rnd 38: K all sts.

Cut yarn, thread through remaining live sts, and pull closed. Pinch top of beak together where the base of it would be (midway between eyes and tip), and, with color A and a darning needle, take a stitch or two at the top to hold it together. The beak is left unstuffed.

• White Patch on Neck (make 2 the same)

The Wood Pigeon has a white patch on both sides of the neck. These are worked flat and then seamed on with the same color. The direction these spots face doesn't matter, as long as both sides are the same. With color D, CO 4 sts to 1 dpn.

Row 1: P all sts.
Row 2: K1, M1L, K2, M1R, K1. (6 sts)
Row 3: P all sts.
Row 4: K all sts.
Row 5: P all sts.
Row 6: SSK, K2, K2tog. (4 sts)
Row 7: P all sts.

Row 8: SSK, K2tog. (2 sts)
Row 9: P all sts.

Cut yarn, thread through last 2 sts, and pull closed. Diagonal lines are now embroidered with colors C and E. These lines are above and slightly over the white patches. Refer to pictures for examples.

• Wings (make 2 the same)

The wings are worked separately, flat at first and then joined in the round. Work begins with the curve at front of wing. With color F, CO 12 sts onto 1 dpn.

Row 1: P all sts.
Row 2: K all sts.
Row 3: P all sts.
Row 4: K9, w&t.
Row 5: P6, w&t.
Row 6: K7, w&t.
Row 7: P8, w&t.
Row 8: K9, w&t.
Row 9: P10, w&t.
Row 10: K11 (EOR).

With RS facing and 2 dpns, begin next to the last st you just knitted and PU 16 sts around the edge of work: 2 sts on each side, and 12 sts along the CO edge. Transfer the first and last of these 16 sts to the original needle. There should now be 14 sts on the first needle, and 7 sts on each of the other two (EOR). Join sts in the round.

Rnd 11: K all sts.
Rnd 12: (K1, M1L, K12, M1R, K1) 2 times. (32 sts)
Rnd 13: K all sts.
Rnd 14: (K1, M1L, K14, M1R, K1) 2 times. (36 sts)

Rnd 15: K all sts.
Rnd 16: (K1, M1L, K16, M1R, K1) 2 times. (40 sts)
Rnds 17–26: K all sts for 10 rounds.
Rnd 27: (K1, K2tog, K14, SSK, K1) 2 times. (36 sts)
Rnds 28–31: K all sts.
Rnd 32: (K1, K2tog, K12, SSK, K1) 2 times. (32 sts)
Rnds 33–36: K all sts.
Rnd 37: (K1, K2tog, K10, SSK, K1) 2 times. (28 sts)
Rnds 38–41: K all sts.
Rnd 42: (K1, K2tog, K8, SSK, K1) 2 times. (24 sts)
Rnds 43–46: K all sts.
Rnd 47: (K1, K2tog, K6, SSK, K1) 2 times. (20 sts)
Rnds 48–51: K all sts.
Rnd 52: (K1, K2tog, K4, SSK, K1) 2 times. (16 sts)
Rnds 53–56: K all sts.
Rnd 57: (K1, K2tog, K2, SSK, K1) 2 times. (12 sts)
Rnds 58–61: K all sts.

Cut color F; join color C.

Rnds 62–63: K all sts.
Rnd 64: (K1, K2tog, SSK, K1) 2 times. (8 sts)
Rnds 65–70: K all sts.
Rnd 71: (SSK, K2tog) 2 times. (4 sts)

Cut yarn, thread through remaining live sts, and pull closed.

• Legs and Feet (make 2 the same)

The legs and feet are made separately and seamed to body. With color A, CO 10 sts to 3 dpns and join in the round.

Rnds 1–2: K all sts.
Rnd 3: (K2tog, K1, SSK) 2 times. (6 sts)
Rnds 4–6: K all sts.

Cut color A; join color G.

Rnd 7: K2tog, K2, SSK (all on 1 dpn). (4 sts)
Rnds 8–11: Work 4 rows of a 4-st I-cord.
Rnd 12: (Kfb) 4 times. (8 sts)
Rnd 13: K2, slide these 2 to other side of dpn.
Rnds 14–17: Work 4 rows of a 2-st I-cord.

Cut yarn, thread through 2 sts, and pull closed. Weave loose end down one side of toe, insert darning needles into bottom of leg and out through color G section; trim.

Rejoin working yarn at next st and repeat rows 13–17 for the next toe, except work 6 rows of a 2-st I-cord instead of 4 since the center toe is slightly longer. Repeat rows 13–17 for the 3rd toe; repeat rows 13–15 for the 4th toe. The last one has only 2 rows of a 2-st I-cord and is the toe that points backward.

Claws can be embroidered or made with a crochet-like chain stitch using black yarn.

NORTH AMERICAN RIVER OTTER

* sighted at San Marcos River San Marcos, Texas

North American river otters have long, muscular streamlined bodies with short legs.

The river otter's eyes and ears are located on its head for surface swimming

Go Bobcats!!

The San Marcos River is normally populated with tubers, boaters, and swimmers. Due to COVID-19 it was closed to most visitors and in the absence of human activity, something remarkable occured - the RETURN of the North American River Otter.

River otters tend to live alone or in pairs, but they socialize in groups and are known for their playful behavior w/ one another.

North American River Otter

SIZE

20"/51 cm long (including tail)
5"/12.5 cm wide

YARN

Cascade Aereo, #4 medium weight, 47% merino wool/31% baby alpaca/22% nylon, 240 yd./220 m per 3.5 oz./100 g skein
- A: 07 Mocha Heather (body, tail, legs, top of head); 180 yd./164 m
- B: 04 Ecru (chest, bottom of head); 40 yd./36.5 m

NEEDLES

US size 5/3.75 mm straight needles
US size 5/3.75 mm dpns

NOTIONS

9 mm black round safety eyes (optional)
Darning needle
Scrap of black yarn to embroider nose
Stitch marker
Stuffing
White thread for whiskers

INSTRUCTIONS

• Chest

Work begins at neckline. The chest is worked with the intarsia method of colorwork. Begin by preparing a second ball of color A (about 20 yards). CO a total of 30 sts onto one straight needle in the following colors and amounts. The chest is worked flat.

Color A: CO 8
Color B: CO 14
Color A: CO 8

Row 1: Color A: P8; Color B: P14; Color A: P8.
Row 2: Color A: K8; Color B: K14; Color A: K8.
Row 3: Color A: P8; Color B: P14; Color A: P8.
Row 4: Color A: K8; Color B: K6, M1L, K2, M1R, K6 (16 sts); Color A: K8.
Row 5: Color A: P8; Color B: P16; Color A: P8.
Row 6: Color A: K8; Color B: K16; Color A: K8.
Row 7: Color A: P8; Color B: P16; Color A: P8.
Row 8: Color A: K8; Color B: K6, M1L, K4, M1R, K6 (18 sts); Color A: K8.
Row 9: Color A: P8; Color B: P18; Color A: P8.
Row 10: Color A: K8; Color B: K18; Color A: K8.

Row 11: Color A: P8; Color B: P18; Color A: P8.
Row 12: Color A: K8; Color B: K6, M1R, K6, M1L, K6 (20 sts); Color A: K8.
Row 13: Color A: P8; Color B: P20; Color A: P8.
Row 14: Color A: K8; Color B: K20; Color A: K8.
Row 15: Color A: P8; Color B: P20; Color A: P8.
Row 16: Color A: K8; Color B: K6, M1L, K8, M1R, K6 (22 sts); Color A: K8.
Row 17: Color A: P8; Color B: P22; Color A: P8.
Row 18: Color A: K8; Color B: K22; Color A: K8.
Row 19: Color A: P8; Color B: P22; Color A: P8.
Row 20: Color A: K9 (9 sts); Color B: K20 (20 sts); Color A: K9 (9 sts).
Row 21: Color A: P9; Color B: P20; Color A: P9.
Row 22: Color A: K10 (10 sts); Color B: K18 (18 sts); Color A: K10 (10 sts).
Row 23: Color A: P10; Color B: P18; Color A: P10.
Row 24: Color A: K11 (11 sts); Color B: K16 (16 sts); Color A: K11 (11 sts).
Row 25: Color A: P11; Color B: P16; Color A: P11.
Row 26: Color A: K12 (12 sts); Color B: K14 (14 sts); Color A: K12 (12 sts).
Row 27: Color A: P12; Color B: P14; Color A: P12.
Row 28: Color A: K13 (13 sts); Color B: K12 (12 sts); Color A: K13 (13 sts).
Row 29: Color A: P13; Color B: P12; Color A: P13.
Row 30: Color A: K14 (14 sts); Color B: K10 (10 sts); Color A: K14 (14 sts).
Row 31: Color A: P14; Color B: P10; Color A: P14.
Row 32: Color A: K15 (15 sts); Color B: K8 (8 sts); Color A: K15 (15 sts).
Row 33: Color A: P15; Color B: P8; Color A: P15.
Row 34: Color A: K16 (16 sts); Color B: K6 (6 sts); Color A: K16 (16 sts).
Row 35: Color A: P16; Color B: P6; Color A: P16.
Row 36: Color A: K17 (17 sts); Color B: K4 (4 sts); Color A: K17 (17 sts).

• Front Legs

Cut color B yarn only. Arrange last set of color A sts (those currently closest to the end of the needle) onto 3 dpns, as you will now be working in the round. Place color B and first set of color A sts onto a piece of scrap yarn.

Place a st marker at beginning of sts on dpns, or arrange sts with a break here to mark the EOR. CO 2 new sts to the tip of the working needle; these will be the first 2 sts in the next round. (19 sts)

Rnd 1: K all sts.
Rnd 2: K all sts.

Rnd 3: K2tog, K15, SSK. (17 sts)
Rnd 4: K all sts.
Rnd 5: K all sts.
Rnd 6: K2tog, K13, SSK. (15 sts)
Rnd 7: K all sts.
Rnd 8: K2tog, K11, SSK. (13 sts)
Rnd 9: K all sts.
Rnd 10: K2tog, K9, SSK. (11 sts)
Rnd 11: K all sts.
Rnd 12: K2tog, K7, SSK. (9 sts)
Rnd 13: K all sts.
Note: Rnds 14–20 below will be repeated for the back legs.
Rnd 14: K2, (Kfb) 5 times, K2. (14 sts)
Rnd 15: K2, (K1, P1) 5 times, K2.
Rnd 16: K2, (K1, P1) 5 times, K2.
Rnd 17: K2, (K1, P1) 5 times, K2.
Rnd 18: K2, SSK, (K1, P1) 3 times, K2tog, K2. (12 sts)
Rnd 19: K2, SSK, (P1, K1) 2 times, K2tog, K2. (10 sts)
Rnd 20: K2, SSK, K1, P1, K2tog, K2. (8 sts)

Cut yarn, thread through remaining live sts, and pull closed. Weave in loose end.

Leaving color B sts on scrap yarn, arrange 1st set of color A sts onto 3 dpns. CO 2 new sts to end. These will be the last 2 sts in the next round. Place a st marker or arrange sts with a break here to mark the EOR (19 sts). Repeat rounds 1–20 and finishing instructions above.

Place the 4 live color B sts onto a dpn.

• Body

Bring first and last CO sts together forming a circle. Seam the top 15 rows together, creating a round opening for the neck.

Sts are now picked up along the edges of the work to begin the body. With RS facing, color A, and 3 dpns, begin picking up a total of 48 sts as follows:

- 1st dpn: PU 16 sts along right edge of chest, beginning just below the seam and working downward to right leg
- 2nd dpn: PU 6 sts across top of right leg, K4 (the live color B sts), PU 6 sts across top of left leg
- 3rd dpn: PU 16 sts along left edge of chest, from left leg upward to the seam (EOR)
  48 sts total. Join sts in the round.

Rnd 1: K all sts.
Rnd 2: K1, M1R, K46, M1L, K1. (50 sts)
Rnds 3–5: K all sts.
Rnd 6: K1, M1R, K48, M1L, K1. (52 sts)

Rnds 7–9: K all sts.
Rnd 10: K1, M1R, K50, M1L, K1. (54 sts)
Rnds 11–13: K all sts.
Rnd 14: K1, M1R, K52, M1L, K1. (56 sts)
Rnds 15–17: K all sts.
Rnd 18: K1, M1R, K54, M1L, K1. (58 sts)
Rnds 19–21: K all sts.
Rnd 22: K1, M1R, K56, M1L, K1. (60 sts)
Rnds 23–25: K all sts.
Rnd 26: K1, M1R, K58, M1L, K1. (62 sts)
Rnds 27–29: K all sts.
Rnd 30: K1, M1R, K60, M1L, K1. (64 sts)
Rnds 31–53: K all sts.

The following 3 sections of short rows will shape the curve in the back and change the direction of the sts to point downward.

Row 54: K6, w&t.
Row 55: P12, w&t.
Row 56: K14, w&t.
Row 57: P16, w&t.
Row 58: K18, w&t.
Row 59: P20, w&t.
Row 60: K22, w&t.
Row 61: P24, w&t.
Row 62: K12 (EOR).
Row 63: K all sts, picking up and knitting the last wrap on the K side, and the last wrap on the P side together with the stitch.

Row 64: K1, K2tog, K4, w&t. (63 sts)
Row 65: P7, P2tog, P4, w&t. (62 sts)
Row 66: K14, w&t.
Row 67: P16, w&t.
Row 68: K9, K2tog, K8, w&t. (61 sts)
Row 69: P11, P2tog, P8, w&t. (60 sts)
Row 70: K22, w&t.
Row 71: P24, w&t.
Row 72: K13, K2tog, K12, w&t. (59 sts)
Row 73: P15, P2tog, P12, w&t. (58 sts)
Row 74: K14 (EOR).
Row 75: K all sts, picking up and knitting the last wrap on the K side and the last wrap on the P side, together with the stitch.
Row 76: K6, w&t.
Row 77: P12, w&t.
Row 78: K7, K2tog, K6, w&t. (57 sts)
Row 79: P9, P2tog, P6, w&t. (56 sts)
Row 80: K18, w&t.
Row 81: P20, w&t.
Row 82: K11, K2tog, K10, w&t. (55 sts)
Row 83: P13, P2tog, P10, w&t. (54 sts)
Row 84: K12 (EOR).
Row 85: K all sts, picking up and knitting the last wrap on the K side and the last wrap on the P side together with the stitch.

• Tail

Setup: K14, place next 26 sts onto a piece of scrap yarn. Arrange the 14 remaining sts on 2 dpns; join in the round with the first 14 sts; K14 (EOR).

Rnds 1–5: K all sts.
Rnd 6: K12, SSK, K2tog, K12. (26 sts)
Rnds 7–8: K all sts.
Rnd 9: K11, SSK, K2tog, K11. (24 sts)
Rnds 10–11: K all sts.
Rnd 12: K10, SSK, K2tog, K10. (22 sts)
Rnds 13–16: K all sts.
Rnd 17: K9, SSK, K2tog, K9. (20 sts)
Rnds 18–21: K all sts.
Rnd 22: K8, SSK, K2tog, K8. (18 sts)
Rnds 23–26: K all sts.
Rnd 27: K7, SSK, K2tog, K7. (16 sts)
Rnds 28–31: K all sts.
Rnd 32: K6, SSK, K2tog, K6. (14 sts)
Rnds 33–36: K all sts.
Rnd 37: K5, SSK, K2tog, K5. (12 sts)
Rnds 38–41: K all sts.
Rnd 42: K4, SSK, K2tog, K4. (10 sts)
Rnds 43–46: K all sts.
Rnd 47: K3, SSK, K2tog, K3. (8 sts)
Rnds 48–51: K all sts.
Rnd 52: K2, SSK, K2tog, K2. (6 sts)
Rnds 53–54: K all sts.

Cut yarn, thread through remaining live sts, and pull closed. Weave in loose end.

• Belly

Place the 26 live sts from scrap yarn onto 3 dpns. Sts can be transferred to 1 dpn after a few rows. With RS facing, rejoin color A yarn at the first st on the right side of the tail and work flat, turning work after each row.

Row 1: SSK, K22, K2tog. (24 sts)
Row 2: P all sts.
Row 3: (K2, K2tog) 6 times. (18 sts)
Row 4: P all sts.
Row 5: (K1, K2tog) 6 times. (12 sts)
Row 6: P all sts.
Row 7: (K2tog) 6 times. (6 sts)
Row 8: Cast off on P side.

• Top of Head

The head is worked flat in two different sections: the top (color A) and the bottom (color B). Work begins with the color A section.

With RS facing, color A, and 2 dpns, begin where color A and B meet on the right side of the body.

PU 9 sts in the original CO sts between there and the center seam, and 9 more sts in the CO sts on the other side of the seam. After working a few rows, all the sts can be arranged onto 1 dpn. 18 sts total (EOR).

Row 1: P all sts.
Row 2: K14, w&t.
Row 3: P10, w&t.
Row 4: K14 (EOR).
Row 5: P all sts.
Row 6: K14, w&t.
Row 7: P10, w&t.
Row 8: K14 (EOR).
Row 9: P all sts.
Row 10: K14, w&t.
Row 11: P10, w&t.
Row 12: K14 (EOR).
Row 13: P all sts.
Row 14: K all sts.
Row 15: P all sts.
Row 16: K all sts.
Row 17: P all sts.
Row 18: K all sts.
Row 19: P all sts.
Row 20: (K1, SSK) 3 times, (K1, K2tog) 3 times. (12 sts)
Row 21: P all sts.

Cut yarn, leaving live sts on dpn. Weave in loose ends.

• Bottom of Head

With RS facing, 3 dpns, and color B, pick up and knit a total of 32 sts as follows:
- 1st dpn: PU 10 sts on right side of color A work (begin at bottom and work upward)
- 2nd dpn: K across 12 live color A sts
- 3rd dpn: PU 10 sts on left side of color A work (begin at top and work downward)

Rows 2–8 are short rows to shape the nose.

Row 1: P all sts.
Row 2: (SSK) 2 times, K13, w&t. (30 sts)
Row 3: P2, w&t.
Row 4: K3, w&t.
Row 5: P4, w&t.
Row 6: K5, w&t.
Row 7: P6, w&t.
Row 8: K15, (k2tog) 2 times. (28 sts)
Row 9: P all sts.
Row 10: (SSK) 2 times, K6, cast off 8 sts, K5, (K2tog) 2 times. (16 sts)

At this point there should be 8 sts on each side of the cast-off sts.

Row 11: P8, CO 8 new sts to the tip of your working needle, P8. (24 sts)
Row 12: (SSK) 2 times, K16, (K2tog) 2 times. (20 sts)
Row 13: P all sts.
Row 14: (SSK) 2 times, slip 1st over last st, continue casting off all sts until 4 sts remain on left dpn, (K2tog, slip first st on needle over last one) 2 times. (1 st)

Cut yarn, and pull through last st. The 8 new sts in row 5 will be directly beneath the cast-off sts in row 4. This hole will form your otter's mouth.

Beginning at right corner of mouth opening, PU 18 sts with color B and 3 dpns (EOR). Join sts in the round; K 5 rounds. Cut yarn, leaving a 10-inch tail.

Arrange sts evenly across 2 dpns that run parallel to each other and straight across the mouth; close with Kitchener stitch.

Attach safety eyes in the color A section about 3 rows up from color B and about 7 sts apart from each other.

Stuff head loosely. Seam cast-off edge to color B section of neck, stuffing firmly just before closing. Keep in mind that an otter's head is more flat than round. Push in mouth pocket.

Embroider nose with black yarn and lines around eyes with color A. Add whiskers with white sewing thread.

• Ears (make 2)

The ears are worked separately and seamed to top of head. With color A, CO 10 sts onto 3 dpns. Join in the round by slipping the first CO st onto the 3rd needle and then pulling the 2nd stitch (formerly the last st) over it and off the needle; 9 sts remain. K 1 round. Cast off all sts; weave in loose end. Using the CO tail, pass darning needle under a few CO sts; cinch to close circle. Seam to head with open side facing forward, about 4 rows behind the eyes and 2 sts up from color B section.

• Back Legs (make 2)

The back legs are worked separately and seamed to bottom of body. With color A, CO 19 sts onto 3 dpns. Join in the round by slipping the first CO st onto the 3rd needle and then pulling the 2nd stitch (formerly the last st) over it and off the needle; 18 sts remain.

Rnd 1: K all sts.
Rnd 2: (K1, K2tog) 6 times. (12 sts)
Rnd 3: K all sts.
Rnd 4: (K2, K2tog) 3 times. (9 sts)
Rnd 5: K all sts.

Work rounds 14–20 of the Front Legs section. Seam CO edge to bottom of otter with CO tail and ribbed side of paw facing forward about 2 sts in front of belly decreases and about 6 sts apart from each other. Stuff top of leg firmly just before closing (the feet are not stuffed).

To stand, otter feet are bent forward and positioned flat on the ground. Front legs should point straight down and be parallel to each other.

Acknowledgments

A heartfelt thank-you to Cascade Yarns for the huge boxes that appeared on my porch regularly over the past several months— each one packed with warm browns, rich golds, flaming reds, and earthy greens. It made my heart skip a beat just to look inside, and winding the skeins was always the dessert of my day. Thanks so much for supporting me while I worked on these designs. Your yarn and your generosity are second to none.

Candi—Much better than trail mix! Thank you.

Pat and Bonnie—Could never have made this beautiful book on my own. I'm so proud of you both.

Mark—Thanks for being the best supporter in the world, every single day in every single way. I love you.

GROUP PHOTO BY BETSY SAILORS (MY OTHER DAUGHTER)

Contributors

SARA KELLNER (PATTERN WRITER)

Sara's greatest loves are her family, animals, and designing knitting patterns; combine those three, and she's in heaven. Sara grew up in the Texas Hill Country, running in the woods behind her house and leaving tiny things for the gnomes that lived in the hollows of old trees. Her mother taught her and her brother Ken to knit one hot Saturday on the front porch (using pencils!), and it has brought her joy ever since.

PAT KELLNER (ILLUSTRATIONS)

Pat is a husband and father. He is a half-decent fly fisherman, amateur bird watcher, baseball purist, and lover of ice cream. He runs a fly-fishing company called Flydrology and the website Texas Freshwater Fly Fishing.

BONNIE KUHL (HANDWRITING AND LAYOUT)

Bonnie is a mom to one boy and two cats. She loves art and illustrations and runs a business called Archer and Olive.